This book belongs to

....

....

....

JAMMU AND KASHMIR

HIMACHAL PRADESH

PUNJAB CHANDIGARH

UTTARAKHAND
178 (161-195)

HARYANA

DELHI

RAJASTHAN
32 (30-35)

UTTAR PRADESH
109 (91-127)

SIKK

BIHAR
10 (7-13)

JHARKHAND
Not Assessed

WEST BENG
10 (8-12)

GUJARAT

MADHYA PRADESH
300 (236-364)

CHHATTISGARH
26 (23-28)

45 (37-53)

ORISSA

DAMAN & DIU
DADRA & NAGAR HAVELI

MAHARASHTRA
103 (76-131)

95 (84-107)

ANDHRA PRADESH

GOA

KARNATAKA
290 (241-339)

PONDICHERRY

TAMIL NADU

KERALA - 76 (56-95)
46 (39-53)

N
W   E
S

0 87.6 175   350   525
Kilometers

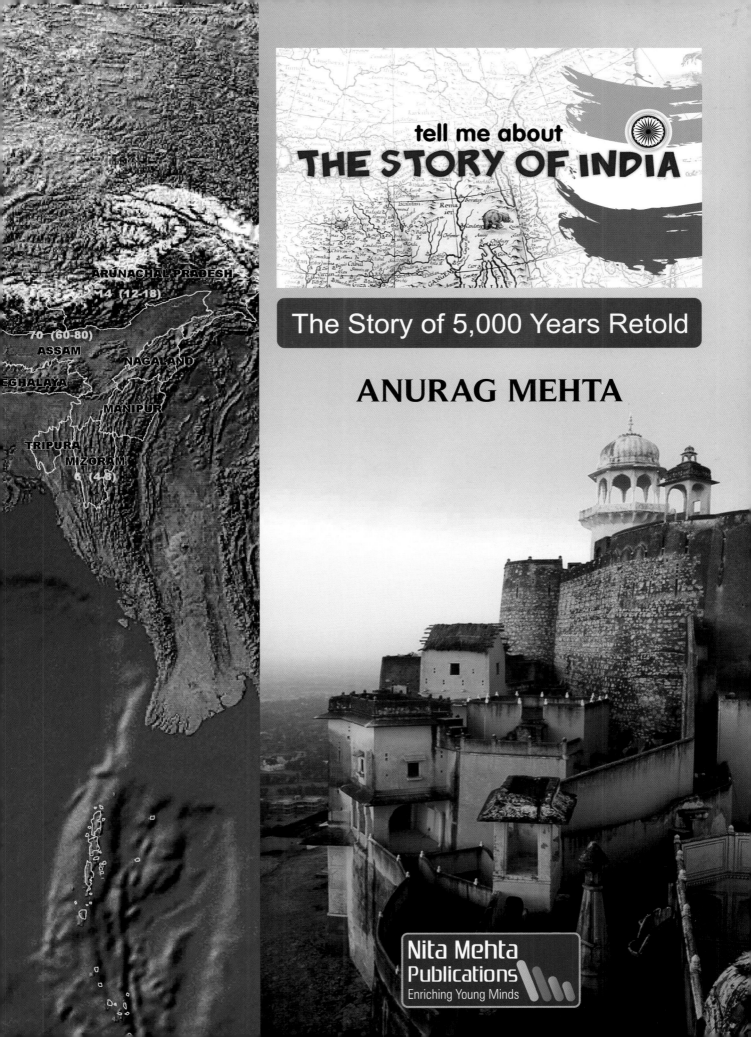

tell me about
THE STORY OF INDIA

The Story of 5,000 Years Retold

ANURAG MEHTA

Nita Mehta
Publications
Enriching Young Minds

The Story of 5,000 Years Retold

Nita Mehta Publications

Corporate Office
3A/3, Asaf Ali Road, New Delhi 110 002
Phone: +91 11 2325 2948, 2325 0091
Telefax: +91 11 2325 0091
E-mail: nitamehta@nitamehta.com
Website: www.nitamehta.com

ISBN 978-81-7676-116-1

First Print 2013

Printed in India at Infinity Advertising Services (P) Ltd, New Delhi

Distributed by :
NITA MEHTA BOOKS
3A/3, Asaf Ali Road, New Delhi - 02

Distribution Centre :
D16/1, Okhla Industrial Area, Phase-I,
New Delhi - 110020
Tel.: 26813199, 26813200
E-mail: nitamehta.mehta@gmail.com

Editorial and Marketing office
E-159, Greater Kailash II, New Delhi 110 048

Typesetting by National Information Technology Academy
3A/3, Asaf Ali Road, New Delhi 110 002

Price: Rs. 495/-   US$: 19.95   UK£: 15.95

CONTENTS

CONTENTS

INTRODUCTION

As they used to say: "History is about chaps and geography about maps," but I am sure you will agree that the description of a country requires much more than that! You want to know how many festivals there are and how they are celebrated; what are the languages and where are they spoken; which is the driest spot and which the wettest of all; who built the Taj Mahal; where is the Lotus Temple; which is the business capital of the country; what does Union Territory mean; what are the names of all the Indian Prime Ministers; what kind of wildlife do we have and where is it; and so on.

India's history is like a great river of time. We start more than 5000 years ago, with the Indus Valley Civilization. History uses A.D. and B.C. with dates, meaning the years 'Before Christ' (B.C.) and the years 'After Christ' (Anno Domini, A.D.).

Through this book you will understand the many-coloured threads that make up our rich heritage, and make us proud of who we are.

HISTORY OF INDIA

INDUS VALLEY CIVILIZATION

The History of India begins with the birth of the Indus Valley Civilization, better known as the **Harappan Civilization**. Long ago, while workers were digging a railway line between Lahore and Karachi (now in Pakistan), they found some bricks of good quality. What they did not realize was that these bricks were about 3,000 years old. Later when the area was dug out, the Archaeological Department of India unearthed the ruins of the two old cities, named Mohenjodaro and Harappa.

This came to be known as the Harappa culture. This civilization flourished more than 4,500 years ago. The cities were well planned, the houses were made of burnt bricks and some were even double storeyed. With public buildings like the **Great Bath**, proper drainage systems and the knowledge of growing cereals, this civilization was more advanced than any other in the world at that point of time.

DID YOU KNOW?
The Great **Bath**, situated in the citadel was a unique structure in Mohenjodaro. This was an oblong bathing pool 39x23 feet in area and 8 feet deep.

By 1500 BC, the Harappan culture came to an end. Among various causes attributed to the decay of Indus Valley Civilization are the invasion by the Aryans, the recurrent floods and other natural causes like earthquake.

VEDIC CIVILIZATION

The Vedic civilization is the earliest civilization in the history of ancient India. It is associated with the coming of Aryans. It is named after the *Vedas*, the early literature of the Hindu people. The **Aryans**, who are believed to have come from the plains of Central Asia, lived in tribes and spoke Sanskrit. They settled along the Indus River at first and later moved on to the Ganges valley. In addition to their language, the Aryans brought their Gods with them to India.

The Aryans were divided into three groups: - The warriors, the priests and the cultivators. This division was on the basis of their occupation and not birth. During this period, a new religion called Hinduism emerged and those who followed it came to be known as Hindus.

As time passed, there were changes in society and a sense of superiority grew in the priest and warrior class. Soon, society was divided into a new system called the 'caste system'. In this the division of people into the different classes was on the basis of birth and not by occupation.

The new classes which emerged were: - the **Brahmins** (the priests), the **Kshatriyas** (the warriors), the **Vaishyas** (the business people), the **Shudras** (the labourers/workers), and the **Untouchables** (lowest caste).

The caste system was rigid and this division of society was very shameful as it promoted the belief that some human beings are better than the others.

Most of the information about the **Aryans** is found in the books called the **Vedas** which are the oldest books in the world and are written in Sanskrit. Also, during the time of the Aryans, two of the greatest epics, **Ramayana** and **Mahabharata** were written.

BUDDHIST ERA

567 BC to 487 BC (more than 2,500 years ago)

Siddhartha Gautama was the son of King Shuddhodana of Kapilavastu and his wife Maya. He grew up to be an unhappy young man. Later in his life, he withdrew from his home and family in search of answers and while doing so, he gained enlightenment. He began to spread his knowledge to other people and soon came to be known as **Buddha**. He thus became the founder of **Buddhism**, the religion and the philosophical system that evolved into a great culture throughout much of southern and eastern Asia.

ALEXANDER'S INVASION

In 326 BC northern India was conquered by **Alexander** the Great, a Macedonian (Greek) king whose dream was to conquer the whole world. Alexander found out that there were two powerful kings in Punjab - Ambhi and Porus. As Alexander moved to Taxila, to fight with Ambhi, Ambhi refused to fight and instead gave his kingdom off to Alexander. He then challenged king Porus, who fought a battle with Alexander but eventually lost. Since his army was tired, Alexander decided to go home and left some Generals behind. But he died on his way back to Babylon (modern Iraq) in 323BC when he was only 33 years old.

DID YOU KNOW?
Q. Which new weapon did Alexander's army meet for the first time in India?
A. Elephants. They fought with elephants, which the Macedonians had never seen before.

THE MAURYAN EMPIRE

321 BC to 298 BC

With news of Alexander's death, his Generals also left India. The confusion following the death of Alexander gave **Chandragupta Maurya** an opportunity to free the country from the clutches of the Greeks, and thus occupy the provinces of Punjab and Sindh. He later overthrew Dhanananda, the king of Magadha with the help of **Chanakya**, a priest who Dhanananda had insulted.

Chandragupta ruled his kingdom for 24 years. He then handed the throne to his son **Bindusara** (298BC to 273BC). Bindusara was an able king and expanded the Mauryan Empire during his 25 year rule, after which his son **Ashoka** was crowned king.

Ashoka emerged not only as the most famous king of the Maurya dynasty, but is also regarded as one of the greatest kings of India and the world. The most important event of Ashoka's reign was the conquest of Kalinga (modern Orissa) which proved to be the turning point of his life. The Kalinga war witnessed terrible manslaughter and destruction. The sufferings and atrocities of the battlefield tore Ashoka's heart. He then became a Buddhist and devoted his life to the welfare of the people.

DID YOU KNOW?
Both, the birthplace and the place of death of Ashoka is Pataliputra, or modern day Patna.

THE DECLINE OF THE MAURYAN EMPIRE

200 BC to AD 300

Ashoka was succeeded by weak rulers. Kalinga, which was conquered by Ashoka, was the first to break away and the others followed. In the beginning of the 1st century AD, a tribe called the **Kushanas** established their authority over the north-west frontier of India. The most famous among the Kushana kings was **Kanishka**. He fought many wars and conquered many kingdoms. His kingdom extended from Central Asia to the borders of Bengal, with his capital being Peshawar. Kanishka like Ashoka also moved towards Buddhism. The Kushana rule continued till the middle of 3rd century AD.

During the decline of the Mauryan Empire, the **Satavahana Kingdom** (225BC to AD 225) rose in the Deccan in southern India. Other powerful kingdoms of the south were the **Cholas**, **Pandyas** and the **Cheras**. As the north was in turmoil, the south was rising in strength.

THE GUPTA EMPIRE

Ad320 to AD 525

The Gupta period has been described as the Golden Age of Indian history. The first famous king of the Gupta dynasty was Ghatotkacha's son **Chandragupta I**. After marrying Kumaradevi, a princess from the royal family of the Lichchhavis, his empire grew and extended over Prayag and Ayodhya. Chandragupta also took upon the title of Maharajadhiraja (King of Kings).

After Chandragupta died, his son Samudragupta (AD 335 - AD 375) took over the reigns of the kingdom and ruled for about fifty years. After a gap of several years, India was once again united as one country. The greatest Gupta king was perhaps Samudragupta's son Chandragupta II (AD 380 - AD 414) also known as **Vikramaditya**, who conquered the extensive territories of Malwa, Gujarat and Kathiawar. Despite his many conquests, Vikramaditya is better remembered for his contribution in the field of music, art and literature.

His court was full of musicians, poets and writers. There were nine people whom he considered the best and called them the **'Navratnas'** (nine gems). The great poet and playwright **Kalidas** was one of them. His 'Abhigyan Shakuntalam' (Shakuntala) is a very famous play.

Vikramaditya was succeeded by his son **Kumaragupta** who was later succeeded by **Skandagupta**. The Gupta kings ruled for over 200 years. Their rule was known as the 'Golden age of Indian history' because of its great advancements in various fields.

DID YOU KNOW?

The Indian numeral system and the decimal system including ZERO are Indian inventions of this period. In astronomy, Aryabhatta, in AD 499, gave calculations of the solar year and the shape and movement of astral bodies with remarkable accuracy.

THE HUNS AD 458 - AD 558

During the reign of the Gupta king Skandagupta, fierce nomads called the **Huns** (a branch of the White Huns emanating from Central Asia) came to India. Hearing about the wealth that India bore, they decided to invade India. Their repeated attacks reduced the strength of the Gupta kingdom and eventually the Gupta Empire broke up into a number of small states. But soon, two native powerful princes, **Yasodharman** of Malwa and **Baladitya** of Magadha crushed their power and put an end to their reign in India.

HARSHVARDHAN

AD 606 - AD 647

Harshavardhana ascended the throne of Thaneshwar and Kannauj on the death of his brother, **Rajyavardhana**. By AD 612 Harshavardhana consolidated his kingdom in northern India. Harshavardhana tried to invade the **Chalukya** kingdom in the Deccan, which was then ruled by **Pulakesin II** but was defeated in battle. Once, a Chinese traveler, **Hiuen Tsang**, was visiting India. He came to meet Harshavardhana. After many discussions with Hiuen Tsang, Harshavardhana decided to take up Buddhism. His rule was gentle and he was always concerned about the welfare of the people.

After Harshavardhana's death, with no heir to his throne, India was once again left without any central paramount/supreme power.

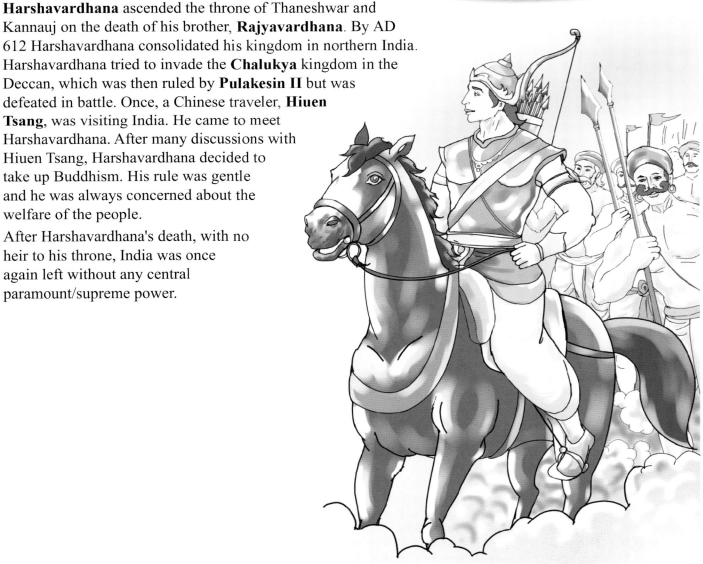

THE SOUTHERN RIVALS

AD 600 - AD 1200

When Harshavardhana was ruling in the north there were three important kingdoms in the south. These were the Chalukyas, the Pallavas, and the Pandyas.

The Chalukyas of Badami

The greatest Chalukya king was Pulakesin II who had even defeated Harshavardhana and stopped him from entering the south. He also defeated the Pallava king Mehendravarman I.

The Pallavas of Kanchi

The Pallava kings were the Tamil kings. In the seventh century their king was Mahendravarman I. The son of Mahendravarman, Narasimhavarman was an even better commander than his father and defeated Pulakesin II whom his father had lost against. This reduced the power of the Chalukyas and in AD 753, the **Rashtrakutas** took over from them.

The Cholas

The Cholas overthrew the Pallavas in the ninth century and became the most powerful kingdom of South India in the eleventh century. This was under the rule of **Rajaraj I** and later his son **Rajendra**.

With the end of the 9th century AD, the medieval history of India started with the rise of empires such as the Palas, the Pratiharas and the Rashtrakutas, and so on.

THE BRAVE RAJPUTS

There were four important Rajput families that ruled in the north. These were the Pratiharas, the Chauhans, the Solankis and the Pawars. The Pratiharas became very powerful during the reign of king Bhoj who ruled from AD 836 to 882. From the Chauhans, there is a very famous king known as **Prithviraj Chauhan**. Prithviraj Chauhan was the last independent Hindu king to sit upon the throne of Delhi.

DID YOU KNOW?
When stories of Prithviraj's courage, valour and intelligence were spreading far and wide, Anangpal, the King of Delhi decided to adopt him. He announced Prithviraj Chauhan as his heir and he was crowned prince of Delhi at the young age of 13 years.

THE INVADERS

The initial entry of Islam into South Asia came in the first century after the death of the Prophet Muhammad. In AD 712, the Arabs attacked Sind under the leadership of Mohammed Bin Kasim. They were able to conquer Sind but could not go further because of the powerful Rajputs of North India.

Three hundred years later, **Sultan Mahmud of Ghazni**, of Afghanistan, decided to raid India. He first attacked the country in AD 1000. Between AD 1000 and 1026, he raided India 17 times and each time the Rajputs failed to stop him. When he finally died in AD 1030, the people of northern India felt relieved.

MUSLIM INVASION OF INDIA

After Mahmud of Ghazni, India did not face any invaders for 160 years. Then in AD 1191, another Turkish invader **Muhammad Ghori** attacked India. He was the ruler of Ghor, a small kingdom in Afghanistan. Unlike Mahmud of Ghazni, Muhammad Ghori not only wanted to take treasures from India, he wanted to conquer North India as well.

The brave Rajput chiefs of northern India headed by Prithviraj Chauhan defeated him in the First Battle of Tarain in 1191 AD. After about a year, Muhammad Ghori came again to avenge his defeat and in the same battlefield, the Rajputs were defeated and Prithviraj Chauhan was captured and put to death. Muhammad Ghori won the throne of Delhi in AD 1192.

THE DELHI SULTANATE

AD 1206 - AD 1413

After Muhammad Ghori died in AD 1206, his Governor **Qutbuddin Aibak** became the Sultan (king) of Delhi. During this period of over three hundred years, five dynasties ruled in Delhi. These were: the Slave dynasty, the Khilji dynasty, the Tughlaq dynasty, the Sayyad dynasty, and finally the Lodhi dynasty.

The Slave Sultans

(AD 1206 to 1290)

The Slave Dynasty ruled the Sub-continent for about 84 years. It was the first Muslim dynasty that ruled India. Qutbuddin Aibak (AD 1206 - 1210) was its first slave king, whose rule lasted for only four years. He was a great builder who built the majestic 238 feet high stone tower known as **Qutab Minar**.

The next important king of the Slave dynasty was **Shams-ud-din Iltutmish** who defeated Qutbuddin Aibak's son to attain the throne. Iltutmish ruled for around 26 years from 1211 to 1235 and was responsible for making the Sultanate of Delhi stronger. After his death his eldest son was declared Sultan but was murdered within seven months of his rule. Then his daughter **Raziya Begum** (AD 1236-1240) took charge and became the only Muslim woman to have adorned the throne of Delhi. Her officers plotted against her as she was a woman and had her killed in AD 1240. After a line of less important rulers, **Balban** a strong and powerful man became the Sultan in AD 1266 and ruled for a number of years.

The Khilji Sultans (AD 1290 to 1320)

Due to Balban's descendants being weak rulers, in AD 1290 a new dynasty of Turkish kings called the Khiljis took over the throne of Delhi. The most famous among their kings was **Alauddin**, who had killed his own uncle Jalauddin to ascend the throne. Alauddin Khilji was the first Muslim ruler whose empire covered almost whole of India up to its extreme south. During his reign of 20 years, Mongol invaded the country several times but were successfully defeated. Allauddin died in AD 1316, and with his death, the Khilji dynasty came to an end.

The Tughlaq Sultans (AD 1320 to 1399)

There was confusion in the kingdom after Alauddin's death till AD 1320. A new family of kings called the Tughlaqs took control over the throne. One of the most important Tughlaq kings was **Muhammad-Bin-Tughlaq**, who was the first to shift his capital from Delhi to Devagiri in Deccan. However, it had to be shifted back within two years because it was not feasible. After his death in AD 1351, his cousin, **Feroz Shah** (AD 1351 - 1388) succeeded him.

After Feroz Shah's death in AD 1338, the Tughlaq dynasty came virtually to an end. Although the Tughlaqs continued to reign till 1412, the invasion of Delhi by **Timur**, a fierce Mongol in AD 1398 may have marked the end of the Tughlaq Empire.

The Sayyad Sultans (AD 1414 to 1451)

The Tughlaq dynasty ended in AD 1413 after which **Khzir Khan**, an officer from Timur's army proclaimed himself as the Sultan of Delhi. He ruled for about 37 years. During his reign there was confusion and revolts. The empire came to an end in AD 1451 with his death.

The Lodhi Sultans (AD 1451 to 1526)

This was followed by the Afghan dynasty, the Lodhis. **Buhlul Khan Lodhi** was the first king and the founder of this dynasty. After him came his second son Nizam Shah was proclaimed the king, under the title of **Sultan Sikander Shah**.

THE NEW RELIGIOUS GROUPS

The Sufis

In the eleventh century, some Muslim saints came to India along with the Turkish invaders. They lived a simple life and mixed with the Hindu saints and gurus and were known as Sufis. One of the popular Sufi saints was **Muin-ud-din Chishti**. The **qawwali** became a popular form of singing in gatherings.

The Bhakti Movement

Another religious movement beside the Sufis, which became popular during this time was the Bhakti (devotion) movement. It was founded by Basava and most of the Bhakti saints were from the non-Brahmin castes. This movement was responsible for many rites and rituals associated with the worship of God by Hindus, Muslims and Sikhs of Indian subcontinent. For example, Kirtan at a Hindu Temple, Qawaali at a Dargah (by Muslims), and singing of Gurbani at a Gurdwara are all derived from the Bhakti movement of medieval India.

THE MUGHAL EMPIRE

Babar (AD 1526 - AD 1530)

Following Sikandar Lodhi's death, his son Ibrahim ascended the throne but was killed at Panipat in AD 1526 by Babar's army. This battle is called the **first battle of Panipat**. Thus came the final collapse of Delhi Sultanate and paved the establishment of Mughal Empire in India.

Babar, the king of Kabul (in Afghanistan) was the first Mughal emperor in India. Babar ruled until AD 1530, and was succeeded by his son Humayun.

Humayun (AD 1530 - 1540 and AD 1555 - AD1556)

The eldest son of Babar, Humayun succeeded his father and became the second emperor of the Mughal Empire. He ruled India for nearly a decade but was ousted by **Sher Shah Suri**, the Afghan ruler. Humayun wandered for about 15 years after his defeat. Meanwhile, Sher Shah Suri died and Humayun was able to defeat his successor, Sikandar Suri and regain the crown of Hindustan. However, soon after, he died in 1556 at a young age of 48 years.

DID YOU KNOW?
Humayun was very superstitious and therefore divided his public offices into four distinct groups for the four elements - Earth for Agriculture, Fire for Military, Water for Canals and waterways and Air for everything else!

Sher Shah Suri (AD 1540 - AD 1545)

An Afghan leader, he took over the Mughal Empire after defeating Humayun in 1540. Sher Shah occupied the throne of Delhi for not more than five years, but his reign proved to be a landmark in the Sub-continent. It was under his rule that the Grand Trunk road from Delhi to Kabul was built. However, Sher Shah did not survive long after his accession on the throne and died in 1545 after a short reign of five years.

Akbar (AD 1556 - AD 1605)

Humayun's heir, Akbar, was born in exile and was only 13 years old when his father died. While Akbar was still young, his guardian Bairam Khan looked over the matters of the state. During this time, the nephews of Sher Shah, Adil and Sikander decided to conquer Delhi and sent an army to fight Bairam Khan. The battle which ensued was fought in 1556 and was on the same battlefield of Panipat where Babar had defeated Ibrahim Lodhi. This is known as the **second battle of Panipat** where the Mughals were once again victorious and the nephews were defeated.

At the age of 18, Akbar took over the kingdom and during his reign, the empire expanded and flourished. By the time Akbar was 26, he had many wives and daughters but no son. He visited a Muslim saint named Salim Chishti who promised him three sons. The promise came true and in honour of the saint, Akbar built a city called Fatehpur Sikri in 1571. After Akbar's death in 1605, nearly 50 years after his ascension to the throne, his son Jahangir was crowned king.

Jahangir (AD 1605 - AD 1627)

Akbar was succeeded by his son, who took the title of Jahangir, meaning "Conqueror of the World". He married Mehrunnisa whom he gave the title of 'Nur Jahan' (light of the world). When Jahangir fell ill, Nur Jahan looked over the matters of the state till he recovered and continued to be an important part of the states functioning. In AD 1627, Jahangir died due to an illness. His son Shah Jahan took over the reigns of the Mughal Empire.

DID YOU KNOW?
Jahangir's real name was Salim!

Shah Jahan (AD 1627 - AD 1658)

Jahangir was succeeded by his second son Khurram in 1628. Khurram took the name of Shah Jahan, i.e. the Emperor of the World. He further expanded his Empire to Kandhar in the North and conquered most of Southern India. The Mughal Empire was at its zenith during Shah Jahan's rule. This was due to almost 100 years of unparalleled prosperity and peace. Shah Jahan has been called the 'architect king'. The **Red Fort** and the **Jama Masjid**, both in Delhi, stand out as towering achievements of both civil engineering and art. Yet above all else, Shah Jahan is remembered today for the **Taj Mahal**, the massive white marble mausoleum constructed for his wife Mumtaz Mahal along the banks of the Yamuna River in Agra.

Aurangzeb (AD 1658 - AD 1707)

When Shah Jahan became weak, his four sons began fighting amongst themselves to decide who ascends the throne. Shah Jahan wanted his eldest son **Dara Shikoh** to be the king but the most capable was his third son Aurangzeb. One day, Aurangzeb defeated his brothers and put his old father in prison and crowned himself king. Shah Jahan remained a prisoner for eight years till his death in 1666 at the age of 74. Aurangzeb ruled for 50 years, matching Akbar's reign in longevity. After his reign of hardships and cruelty to his subjects, Aurangzeb died in 1707, at the age of 90 years. With his death, the forces of disintegration set in and the mighty Mughal Empire began collapsing.

THE BRAVE MARATHAS

During the time when Aurangzeb ruled, the Mughal Empire included the whole of north India, central India and part of south India. Around this time a powerful Maratha leader in the Deccan named **Shivaji** was becoming a strong force.

Born in 1627, Shivaji was brought up by his mother **Jijabai**, as his father, an officer in the army was away most of the time. One day, when he was older, he attacked soldiers carrying some treasure from Kalyan to Bijapur, and ran away with the loot. When the Sultan of Bijapur came to know of this, he sent Afzal Khan, one of his Generals, to kill Shivaji. Shivaji came to know about this plan and in turn managed to kill Afzal Khan himself. Shivaji's power was increasing and in order to thwart this, Aurangzeb's General, Jai Singh, managed to capture Shivaji and take over his forts.

Shivaji was then insulted in Aurangzeb's court and later thrown in prison. But he managed to escape. After reaching the Deccan he began to build up his army again and attacked the Mughals. His strategy was to never get into open battle with them but to raid the camps with surprise attacks.

Shivaji was then crowned the king of the Marathas in 1674. When he died in 1680, at the age of 53, he was the ruler of a large, independent state.

THE FALL OF THE MUGHAL EMPIRE AD 1707 to AD 1739

After Aurangazeb's death, his son and successor, Bahadur Shah Zafar, was already old when he took the throne and was confronted with one rebellion after another. Jahadar Shah succeeded him but was later overthrown by Farrukhsiyar. In 1719 Farrukhsiyar was killed and Muhammad Shah came to the throne.

Due to his flippant and merry making nature and lack of stability, he was better known as 'Muhammad Shah Rangila'. The power of the Mughal Empire was further weakened by attacks of the Persian ruler Nadir Shah. The invasion of Nadir Shah was a deathblow to the Mughal Empire.

THE MARATHAS BECOME STRONGER AD 1689 to AD 1761

After Shivaji's death, his son Shambhuji ascended the throne. In 1689 he was captured and killed by a small Mughal army. Shambhuji's son Shahu was taken prisoner by Aurangzeb, but the Marathas did not give up. Shambhuji's brother Rajaram took over the throne and when he died in AD 1700, his wife Tarabai continued to fight the Mughals.

Shahu became the king in 1708 and during his fight to become king, a clever Brahmin named Balaji Vishwanath helped him. For this, Balaji was appointed the Peshwa (chief minister). After Balaji's death his son Baji Rao I (the first) became the Peshwa. After Shivaji, Baji Rao I was the greatest Maratha ruler.

Balaji Baji Rao took over the post of Peshwa from his father in 1740. After nine years, when Shahu died, his son Rajaram took over. As he was a weak ruler, in 1750, Balaji Baji Rao took control and put Rajaram in prison.

The Afghan ruler Ahmad Shah Abdali fought with the Marathas and conquered Punjab. Determined to avenge this defeat, Balaji Rao and Ahmad Shah's armies met at Panipat on 14th January 1761. This battle is known as the **third battle of Panipat**. The Marathas were badly defeated and Balaji himself died of grief some months later.

After the death of Balaji Baji Rao, the Maratha chiefs began to fight among themselves. The kingdom then broke up into five independent states.

THE BRITISH IN INDIA

In the 17th Century

After many had come and gone from Indian shores, the last to arrive and stay were the British. They came and ruled over India for nearly 200 years.

The Arabs had been trading with India for centuries using a sea route. In 1498, a Portuguese sailor named **Vasco da Gama** sailed around Africa and reached Calicut (now Kozihikode) on India's west coast. This discovery of sea route led to many Portuguese ships sailing to India. Soon, the Portuguese captured the port of Goa. The other traders from Europe saw what the Portuguese had done and decided to do the same.

DID YOU KNOW?

The famous 'Battle of Plassey' (23 June 1757) was a decisive (for the British East India Company) victory over the Nawab of Bengal and his French allies, establishing Company rule in South Asia (which expanded over much of the Indies) for the next 190 years.

In 1600, a small group of British traders formed a company called the **East India Company**. Their first ships landed at Surat. In 1615, the British obtained permission from the then Mughal Emperor Jahangir to start trading. The French also continued setting up trade here. Whenever war would break out in the country, the British and French took sides, and eventually made the king who had asked them for help their puppet. The British fought with Siraj-ud-daulah, the Nawab (king) of Bengal. With no consent from him, the British decided to overthrow him and place a puppet king instead. They chose Mir Jaffar, a wicked uncle of Siraj-ud-daulah for his purpose. The traitor uncle did not help while a battle ensued between the British and Siraj-ud-daulah. Finally after Siraj-ud-daulah's defeat Mir Jaffar took over. But he was a ruler only by name. It was the British who controlled him.

Robert Clive, the leader of the British force became the first **Governor of Bengal**. In 1767 when he left India, the British who had initially come as traders, had now become the rulers of a large and prosperous region of India.

TIPU SULTAN AD 1782 to AD 1799

During the time when the British were becoming powerful in India, the state of Mysore (in south India) was ruled by a brave king name Hyder Ali. In 1776 he attacked the kingdom of Malabar and fought with the British. The British signed a treaty by which they agreed to help him if he was attacked by any other ruler. Two years later, the Marathas attacked Hyder Ali, but the British did not help him. In 1780 when he captured Arcot, the British Governor general Warrren Hastings sent an army from Bengal. After being defeated in several battles, Hyder Ali died in 1782 and his son Tipu continued the war.

Tipu Sultan became more dangerous to the British than his father. In 1789, Tipu Sultan attacked Travancore (a state in the south) but this kingdom had the support of the British. The war with this kingdom went on for two years and finally a peace treaty was signed after Tipu Sultan's defeat. In 1799 Tipu Sultan died while defending his capital, Seringapatnam from the combined attack of the Marathas, the Nizam of Hyderabad and the British.

THE REVOLT AGAINST BRITISH RULE

AD 1856 to AD 1858

After the fall of Tipu Sultan, the British had only one powerful rival, the Marathas. But soon the Marathas were also defeated by the British. Victorious in many battles, the British had occupied many areas. After the battle of Plassey in 1757, the British achieved political power in India. Their dominance was established during the tenure of **Lord Dalhousie**, who became the Governor General in 1848. By 1856, while the British established themselves firmly, there was resentment brewing from the Indian populace.

The Indian Mutiny of 1857

In 1857, a new rifle was introduced in the army. Its cartridge had a greased paper cover. The end of the cover had to be bitten off before the cartridge could be loaded into the rifle. The grease was made of mixed animal fat which offended both the Hindu and the Muslim soldiers. The soldiers started revolting and this revolt was known as the **First War of Independence**.

Rani Lakshmibai, the ruler of Jhansi, led her troops in the heroic battles against the British. The Hindus, the Muslims, the Sikhs and all the other brave sons of India fought shoulder to shoulder to throw out the British. The British had control over the revolt within one year. It began from Meerut on 10 May 1857 and ended in Gwalior on 20 June 1858.

DID YOU KNOW?
Rani Lakshmi Bai became a national heroine and was seen as the epitome of female bravery in India. When the Indian National Army created its first female unit, it was named after her.

INDIA AWAKENS AD 1858 to AD 1900

Following the failure of the Revolt of 1857, came the end of the East India Company's rule in India. India was now going to be ruled by the monarch of Britain, Queen Victoria. With no say in the running of the country, the people of India became more resentful of the British. This increasing tension gave rise to the birth of Indian National Movement.

The leadership of the freedom movement passed into the hands of reformists like **Raja Rammohan Roy, Swami Vivekananda, Swami Dayanand Saraswati, Bankim Chandra, Ishwar Chandra Vidyasagar, Annie Besant** and **Sir Syed Ahmad Khan**.

Formation of Indian National Congress (INC)

In 1885 an organisation called the **Indian National Congress** was born. The educated Indians came together and decided to form an organisation. A retired British official by the name of **A. O. Hume** is often referred to as the father of the INC. The congress soon spread all over the country. One of the most important leaders during its earliest days was **Dadabhai Naoroji**. He declared that India's goal was Swarajya or Freedom.

Many other leaders played an important part during the freedom struggle like Surendranath Banerjee and Gopal Krishna Gokhale. Of them were a group of leaders popularly known as **Bal-Pal-Lal** or Bal Gangadhar Tilak, Bipin Chandrapal and Lala Lajpat Rai.

Tilak took up the people's cause by publishing articles in his newspaper **Kesari**. Following this, two British officers were shot and killed and Tilak was sentenced to 18 months' imprisonment. When he emerged from prison, he was honored as a martyr and a national hero and adopted a new slogan, "Swaraj (Freedom) is my birth right and I shall have it." Tilak wanted to make every man participate in the freedom struggle.

Soon, the British decided to use the policy of Divide and Rule in India in which they decided to divide Bengal into two halves. One half would have the Muslims while the other, Hindus. The Congress decided to take action against this decision. The Congress now had two parts - the Moderates led by Dadabhai Naoroji, Gopal Krishna Gokhale and Feroz Shah Mehta and the Extremists led by Tilak, Lajpat Rai and Bipin Chandrapal. The two groups were united to oppose the partition of Bengal. The Swadeshi and the Boycott Movements were started in which the people boycotted (stopped using) all foreign goods and used only those made in India (Swadeshi goods).By 1906, the Muslims had also established an organization for themselves and called it the Muslim League.

FREEDOM MOVEMENT AD 1919 to AD 1948

Two freedom fighters who motivated the Indians to fight for freedom during this time were **Chandrashekhar Azad** and **Bhagat Singh**. But aside from them there is one man whose name can never be forgotten in Indian history. Born **Mohandas Karamchand Gandhi**, this man grew to be the father of the nation. As a lawyer in South Africa for 22 years, Gandhi fought for justice. In 1915, he returned to India.

During this time, the First World War broke out where the Indian soldiers helped the British under the conditions of better reforms once the war was over. But the response from the British end was unsatisfactory and Gandhiji asked the soldiers to break the new reforms. At this, the British arrested thousands of people while killing hundreds.

Jallianwala Bagh

The most brutal attack by the British was perhaps the Jallianwala Bagh massacre. On 13th April 1919, at a place called **Jallianwala Bagh** in Punjab, 20,000 men and women gathered to listen to their leaders during the time when the British had declared public meetings to be illegal. The British officer General Dyer decided to teach Indians a lesson by coming armed to the meeting, blocking all exits to the ground and opening fire. With no escape route for the people and non-stop firing, over 1,000 people were killed while 1,200 were wounded. After this attack, Gandhiji declared Satyagrah (force of truth) against the British.

Non Cooperation Movement

Under the leadership of Mahatma Gandhi, the Congress launched a series of mass movements - the **Non-Cooperation Movement** of 1920-1922 and the **Civil Disobedience Movement** in 1930. The Non-Cooperation Movement was triggered by the famous Salt (Dandi) March. The aim of the Civil Disobedience movement was a complete disobedience of the orders of the British Government.

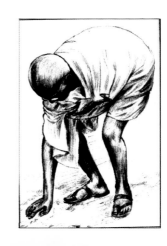

Quit India Movement

In August 1942, Gandhiji started the **'Quit India Movement'** and decided to launch a mass civil disobedience movement, a 'Do or Die' call to force the British to leave India. While this was happening, the Muslim League under the leadership of **Muhammad-Ali-Jinnah** declared that Muslims were separate people and must have their own country called **Pakistan**.

Meanwhile, **Netaji Subhash Chandra Bose**, who stealthily ran away from the British detention in Calcutta, reached foreign lands and organized the Indian National Army (INA) to overthrow the British from India.

India - Pakistan Partition

In 1946, the British government announced that they were willing to end their rule in India. The Muslim League pressed its demand for a separate country for Muslims. The difference between the Hindus and Muslims could no longer be resolved. With many riots taking place and many people dying, all efforts to keep India united seemed unsuccessful.

Thus, India became independent on 15 August, 1947. A separate country called Pakistan was created, while Pandit Jawahar Lal Nehru became the first prime minister of India. Even as everyone else enjoyed a peaceful phase in their lives, Gandhiji was busy comforting victims of the Hindu-Muslim riots. On 30th January 1948, Gandhiji was shot dead while he was on his way to attend his evening prayers in Delhi. Affectionately called 'Bapu', (which means father in Hindi), Gandhiji lived and died for his country and will be remembered as the father of the nation.

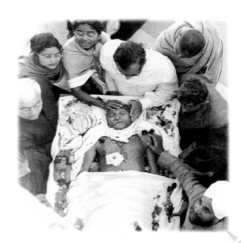

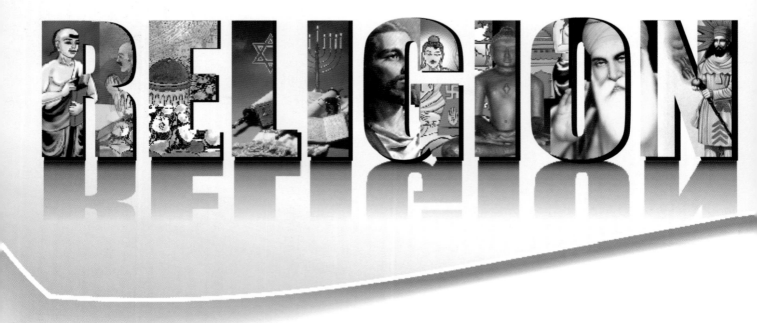

RELIGIONS OF INDIA

India has been an important part of three major world religions - Hinduism, Buddhism and Islam.

HINDUISM

The coming of the Aryans marked the beginning of the religious tradition known as Hinduism. It is the only religion which cannot be traced to a specific founder and the only one which does not have a singular 'holy book' as the one and only scriptural authority.

Those who practice Hinduism are known as **Hindus**. The first written evidence of Hinduism is the **Rig Veda**, a long poem in Sanskrit probably composed about 1000 BC. People sang or recited this before it was written down around 300 BC. Earlier the nature Gods were worshipped (i.e. Fire, Wind, Water etc.), later came other Gods like Shiva and Vishnu and finally the mother Goddesses.

Hindus believe in the concept of reincarnation. In Hinduism a holy **trinity of Gods** comprising of **Brahma** (the creator), **Vishnu** (the preserver) and **Shiva** (the destroyer) are the most sacred. Each God in the trinity has his companion. To Brahma is **Saraswati**, the Goddess of knowledge. For Vishnu is **Lakshmi**, the Goddess of wealth, beauty and delight. For Shiva is Kali (Parvati), the Goddess of power, destruction and transformation.

The place of worship for Hindus is known as a temple or '*mandir*'. A Hindu temple can be a separate structure or a part of a building. A feature of most temples is the presence of '*murtis*' or idols of the Hindu deity to whom the temple is dedicated. However, some temples are dedicated to several deities, and some have symbols instead of a *murti*.

BUDDHISM

As mentioned earlier in the book, Siddhartha Gautama, the son of King Shuddhodana of Kapilavastu became **Lord Buddha** or the Fully Awakened One. He meditated under a *peepul* tree near Bodh Gaya, where he attained Bodhi (Enlightenment). The tree that had sheltered him came to be known as the Bodhi tree. Lord Buddha died at the age of 80 in 487BC.

The Buddha was born in India and even died there. His teachings were imparted in the context of his Indian heritage. A thousand years after his death, he was accepted as an incarnation of Vishnu. And while Buddhism remained an Indian religion for many centuries, it soon became an Asian one.

Many came to follow his teachings and became monks and nuns. Thus, the new religion Buddhism was born. **Buddhists** believe that everyone is reborn after death but the quality of their next life is dependant on their deeds (karma) in the present life. Buddhists aim to achieve absolute peace, a state which they call Nirvana by following the Eight-Fold Path of the good life.

In the 3rd century BC the emperor Ashoka also became a Buddhist. His conversion marked the expansion of Buddhism. At first, most Buddhists were in India. But soon Buddhism spread to China and other parts of East Asia.

The place of worship for Buddhists is called a Buddhist Temple. Inside the temple, there is a shrine and often a statue of the Buddha either meditating or lying down.

DID YOU KNOW?
One of the interesting facts about Buddha is that Gautam Buddha's disciple Ananda, Buddha's wife, and his chariot rider were born on the same day i.e. when He was born!! Surprisingly the peepal tree where he achieved the Nirvana was also planted on the same day!!

JAINISM

About the same time as Buddha was preaching his dharma, in the same region, another religious tradition was being established by Vardhamana, better known by his title **Mahavir** ("Great Hero"). After attaining knowledge, Mahavir was called Jin which means the 'conqueror of the soul' and started the religion of Jainism. His teachings became popular and those who followed him came to be known as **Jains**.

Jainism has 24 religious Trihankara or the lords to guide the devotees in the world. Trihankaras are born as humans and are considered to be Gods in the Jain community. Mahavir was born to Siddhartha of Kundanpur and his wife Trisala. Before his birth, Mahavir's mother saw many dreams which told her that the baby was a Trihankara. At the age of thirty, Mahavir left his home and wandered seeking the truth about life and existence. After giving up all his possessions and clothes, Mahavir meditated under an Ashoka tree and gained enlightenment.

There are two Jain philosophies - Svetembara and Digambara. Digambara monks like Mahavir don't wear any clothes, but normally they don't walk like that outside their temples. The Digambaras include only men. The Svetembara monks wear white clothes and include women.

A derasar is a temple for followers of Jainism. Jain idols of Tirthankaras usually built from marble are worshipped there. Some famous Jain temples are located in Palitana, Shankeshwar, Shikharji, Vataman, Mumbai, and Ahmedabad.

ISLAM

The word Islam means "submission" or the total surrender of oneself to God (Arabic: *Allah*). A follower of Islam is known as a **Muslim**, meaning 'one who submits to God'.

In the year AD 570, a great man was born in a little town called Mecca in Arabia. His name was **Mohammed**. While Mohammed was growing up, Arabia was full of warring tribes. Muslims believe that God revealed the **Quran/Koran** to Muhammad, God's final prophet. They regard the Quran/Koran and the *Sunnah* (words and deeds of Muhammad) as the fundamental sources of Islam. In AD 622 Mohammed left Mecca and went to Medina, a nearby town. After eight years the Prophet returned to Mecca and defeated the tribes that had harassed and threatened him. He died in AD 632.

The basic injunctions of Islam are summed up in the 'Five Pillars' which are five duties that unite Muslims into a community. In general the Muslims of India like the Muslim world are divided into two main sects, Sunni and Shia. Those Muslims who claim to be the descendants from the daughter of Prophet Muhammad and the men in this community add the title *Syed* before their names. Others claim to be the descendants from the first Muslims and add the title Sheik. Another important part of early Islam was Sufism, which was a belief in a direct relationship between people and God shared by many Sunnis and Shiites.

The main place of worship for Muslims is a **Mosque** where there is a prayer hall. There is no furniture, only mats and carpets to pray on. On one wall there is a platform which shows the direction of the *Kaaba*. There are no pictures of Allah or Mohammad or even animals in the Mosque. Instead the walls and ceilings are decorated with beautiful patterns and writing.

DID YOU KNOW?
The Kaaba (the Cube) is a cube-shaped building in Mecca, Saudi Arabia, and is the most sacred site in Islam. The building has a mosque built around it and all Muslims around the world face the Kaaba during prayers, no matter where they are.

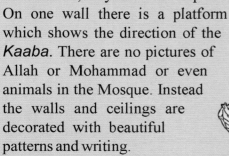

SIKHISM

This religion was established by **Guru Nanak** who was born into a Hindu family in 1469 in the Punjab region. Since childhood he loved to travel, learn and preach humanity. In those days people who taught and preached were titled Guru meaning teacher, his followers became to be known as Sikhs meaning learners or disciples. In Sikhism everyone has equal rights irrespective of caste, creed, color, race, sex or religion. Sikhism rejects pilgrimage, fasting, superstitions and other such rituals and believe that there is a single, all-powerful God, who created the universe and everything in it.

Guru Nanak who established Sikhism was its first Guru. Angad, who succeeded Nanak as the Guru of the Sikhs, started compiling the masters' writings. He also introduced a script which was already being used by some Punjabis. He called it **Gurmukhi** and made it the official script of the Sikhs. After him there were eight more Gurus. The last Guru, **Guru Gobind Singh**, proclaimed that after him the Guru of the Sikhs would be the holy book of Sikhism, **Guru Granth Sahib** (the Book of the Lord).

Guru Gobind decided to make his followers, the Sikhs, a community of fighters. He changed his surname to **Singh**, which means lion. His followers did the same. Since then a ceremony of baptizing was established among the Sikhs in which the boys were given the title Singh and the girls were titled Kaur meaning princess. In order to make it easier for his followers to recognize each other, Gobind Singh, chose five marks, some of which even today symbolize the Sikhs. The five signs were, uncut hair; comb; sword or dagger; bracelet on the right wrist and shorts.

A Sikh place of worship is called **Gurdwara** meaning 'the doorway to the Guru'. Sikhism does not support pilgrimage to holy sites because according to Sikhism, God is everywhere and not in any certain place. But Sikhism has a few important sites, of which, the Hari Mandir, also known as the **'Golden Temple'** in Amritsar in Punjab is the most important site and is considered the holiest shrine of Sikhism.

CHRISTIANITY

Christianity is a religion centered on the life and teachings of Jesus of Nazareth as recounted in the New Testament. Its followers, known as **Christians** or the 'disciples of Christ,' believe **Jesus** to be the Son of God and the Messiah (or Christ) prophesied in the Old Testament. To Christians, Jesus Christ is not merely a teacher and the model of a pious life but the revealer of God, the mediator of salvation and the saviour who suffered, died and was resurrected in order to bring about salvation from sin for all.

Christianity arrived in India almost about the same period as it arrived in Europe, about 2000 years ago. Christianity originates in Israel. The first Christians were Jews. Of the original 12 disciples called by Jesus to preach the gospel, it is said that St. Judas Thomas, arrived in India and converted Indians to Christianity. A carpenter and a disciple of Jesus, he was brought to India by a merchant to build a temple. St. Thomas arrived in Kerala, in south India in 52 AD. He succeeded in converting local Indians to Christianity. But most of the Indian were converted to Christianity by the missionaries who arrived in India with the European powers in the 15th century.

Christianity regards the **Bible**, a collection of books in two parts (the Old Testament and the New Testament), as authoritative. The **cross**, which is today one of the most widely recognized symbols in the world, was used as a Christian symbol from the earliest times.

The place of worship for Christians is called the **church**. The main division of Christians in India is like in the Christian world, Protestants and Catholic. The major centers of Christianity in India are Kerala, Tamil Nadu, Goa, Manipur and Mizoram. There is also a big community of Christians in Mumbai.

ZOROASTRIANISM

Zoroastrianism is the religion and philosophy based on the teachings ascribed to the prophet Zoroaster (Zarathustra). In India, it exists mostly as a small religious community in Mumbai. The follower of Zoroastrianism is called a **Parsi** because the religion arrived in India from Persia. The followers of this religion were exiled from Iran in the 7th century AD, because of religious attacks by the Muslims. They arrived in the Gujarat region of India.

The holiest place for them is the village of **Udvada** in Gujarat, India. The holy language of the Parsis is an ancient language spoken in Iran, Avesta. Parsis believe that there is one universal and transcendental God, **Ahura Mazda**, the representative of God. For them fire, water, air and earth are pure elements to be preserved and therefore they do not cremate or bury their dead ones but leave them on high towers, specially built for this purpose, to be eaten by hawks and crows. The religions main tenets are about the struggle between good and evil.

The holy place of worship of the Parsis is the fire temple known as the **agiary** or dar-be mehr. The latter is the Gujarati language word for 'house of fire'. They believe that Zoroaster brought the sacred fire from heaven to earth and therefore this fire is kept burning by the high priest of the agiary.

JUDAISM

Judaism is the religion of the **Jewish** people, based on principles and ethics embodied in the **Hebrew Bible** (Tanakh), as further explored and explained in the Talmud. The Talmud is a record of discussions pertaining to Jewish law, ethics, customs, and history. According to Jewish tradition, the history of Judaism begins with the contract between God and Abraham, the patriarch and founder of the Jewish people. Judaism is among the oldest religious traditions still in practice today. Jewish history and doctrines have influenced other religions such as Christianity and Islam.

The Jews of India aren't one singular community. Among themselves they are divided into different communities, each with its own culture, background and origin. There is no clarity on how these communities really came to India. Judaism was one of the first non-Dharmic religions to arrive in India in recorded history.

The three main Jewish communities of India are: Bene Israel, Cochini and Baghdadi. Besides these, are the Bene Ephraim also called Telugu Jews and a community in east India which claim Israeli origin and call themselves Beni Menashe.

The place of worship for Jews is a **synagogue**. Their holy day starts on Friday evening and goes to Saturday night. Men and women sit separately in some synagogues. Inside there are the Torah scrolls. There is a large cupboard called an Ark on top of which is a light which is never put out.

MYTHOLOGY

Two great epic poems, the **Ramayana** and the **Mahabharata** written during the earlier times are interwoven into the fabric of Hinduism. The most popular texts in the Vedic tradition, called the **Bhagavad Gita** (Song of God) is a part of the Mahabharata.

Ramayana

The story of the Ramayana is simple enough. Rama, eldest son of King Dasharatha of Ayodhya, was banished for 14 years through his stepmother's scheming. He went into the forest, accompanied by his wife Sita and younger brother, Lakshmana. Sita was kidnaped and taken to Sri Lanka on the orders of the demon-king, Ravana. Rama, supported by an army of monkeys led by Hanuman, defeated Ravana and rescued his wife. Rama, an incarnation of Vishnu, emerges from the epic as the perfect man.

Mahabharata

The Mahabharata revolves around the conflict between the five Pandava brothers and their cousins, the Kauravas, who had wrongly seized their kingdom. Krishna, an incarnation of God, became the advisor of Arjuna, the commander of the Pandava army. On the eve of the battle between the two sides, Arjuna, one of the Pandava brothers, was plagued with doubt and refused to fight against his own kin. Krishna then spoke to him and told him to fight for justice and the truth. This battle was declared a war between good and evil. In the end, the Pandavas were victorious and justice prevailed.

FESTIVALS OF INDIA

Festivals in India are characterized by colour, gaiety, enthusiasm, prayers and rituals. No wonder, India is described as the Land of Festivals.

In India there are two types of calendars used other than the **Roman calendar**. They are the **Hindu calendar** and the *Hijri* or the **Islamic calendar**. Both are lunar calendars i.e. they are based on the movement of the moon. Festivals in India occur throughout the year due to the diverse cultures and religions that follow their own calendar.

Let's find out a little about the festivals in order of the month based on the Roman calendar, which is from January till December.

LOHRI

The festival of Lohri marks the end of winter and the onset of spring. Celebrated on the **13th of January** every year, Lohri is one of the most important festivals celebrated in **Punjab**, **Haryana** and parts of **Himachal Pradesh**, where agriculture is the main occupation. Lohri is a celebration of a bountiful crop in the field, promising wealth and prosperity.

After this day, the winter chill declines and the days start becoming longer and warmer. In the evenings, a bonfire is lit in an open area in front of people's homes and one is supposed to go around the fire before starting the celebration. Seasonal savouries and sweets like popcorn, rewari, gajak, peanuts and sugar cane are eaten.

According to Punjabi folklore, Lohri was celebrated to mark the longest night of the year - for the day after Lohri would only bring increasing daylight. The origin of Lohri is related to the central character of most Lohri songs on *Dulla Bhatti* who was really a dacoit (but on the lines of Robin Hood). To this day many songs highlighting his heroic deeds are sung during Lohri celebrations.

PONGAL

On the **14th of January** (one day after Lohri), when there are newly harvested rice grains, a dish is prepared. Sesame seeds, jaggery, chickpeas, groundnuts and dried coconut are added to the rice grains. These ingredients are put into a pot of milk and boiled till the milk spills over. This delicious dish is called **Pongal**. Pongal actually means **'boiled over'**. This festival is popular in South India particularly Tamil Nadu and Andhra Pradesh.

Originally Pongal was a harvest festival which fell on the same day as Makar Sankranti, which is why it is sometimes called Pongal Sankranti. Pongal is a four day festival. On the first day, people pray to the Rain God, on the second they pray to Surya or the Sun God. A cow is worshipped on the third day and finally, on the fourth day, nothing new is started and people just relax or visit family members.

MAKAR SANKRANT

Makar Sankranti is an important Hindu religious festival celebrated on the **14th of January** each year, one day after the festival of Lohri. The festival is a counterpart of Pongal in South India. On this day, it is traditional to take a dip in the holy Ganges and pray for our ancestors.

On Makar Sankranti, devotees bathe in the river Ganga (Ganges) before sunrise, they pray to the rising sun and chant the Gayatri Mantra while offering flowers. Charity to the needy in the form of rice and dal is distributed.

In Punjab, Makar Sankranti is called Lohri and is celebrated to rejoice the harvest. In Bengal, the huge Ganga Sagar mela commences while in Gujarat, it is the time for kite flying. In Maharashtra people exchange 'til' *ladoos* and in the south this is called Pongal.

DID YOU KNOW?

In Punjab, Makar Sankranti is called Lohri and is celebrated to rejoice the harvest. In Bengal, the huge Ganga Sagar Mela commences while in Gujarat, it is the time for kite flying. In Maharashtra people exchange 'til' ladoos and in the south this is called Pongal.

BASANT PANCHAMI

Basant or 'Vasant' means the season of **spring**. This is the season of the farmers cheering as they see the fields dancing with mustard flowers during the time of bloom and growth. This festival is termed as the first day of spring. The Goddess of Knowledge, **Goddess Saraswati** is worshiped today.

On this day, children and adults perform Saraswati Puja (worship of Goddess Saraswati) and pray for wisdom and knowledge. The Goddess bestows the gifts of education, dance, music, arts on people. People wear yellow clothes and even prepare delicacies in the same colour because this is the season of yellow mustard.

Married women, apart from wearing yellow clothes even adorn their hands with yellow bangles. This festival ushers in the spring season with music, dance and frolic.

MAHA SHIVRATRI

The festival of Maha Shivratri symbolizes the wedding day of the Hindu Gods, Lord Shiva and Parvati. This festival comes some time in February or March, 14-15 days before Holi. Individuals fast and stay awake through the night praying to Shiva. The chanting of Om Namash Shivai rings the air. Shiv temples are beautifully decorated.

The fast is broken the next morning as hymns are sung throughout the night in praise of Shiva. People believe that all their sins will be washed away if they pray with proper devotion to Shiva on Maha Shivratri.

According to one legend, during the churning of the ocean, a deadly pot of poison was thrown up. This disturbed the Gods and demons because the poison was so venomous it could destroy the world and mankind. Shiva agreed to swallow this poison and save the world. When he swallowed the poison his throat became blue as the poison was so toxic. He was given the name *Neel Kantha* or the blue throated one! This event is believed to be celebrated as Maha Shivratri, the day Shiva saved the world.

ID-UL-ZUHA

Id-ul-Zuha (Bakr-Id), a festival of Muslims, is celebrated with great joy, special prayers and exchange of greetings and gifts. It falls on the tenth day of the twelfth month of the **Islamic calendar**. Id-ul-zuha, the festival of sacrifice comes from the word 'Id' derived from the Arabic 'iwd' meaning 'festival' and 'Zuha' comes from 'uzhaiyya' which translates to 'sacrifice'.

This festival is celebrated to mark the ordeals faced by the **Prophet Ibrahim**, four thousand years ago. According to legend, Prophet Ibrahim was put to a tough test to prove his loyalty towards *Allah* even though he was very devoted and followed all his instructions with dedication. One day, Allah came in Ibrahim's dreams and told him to sacrifice his son Ismail to show his loyalty. Without hesitation, both Ibrahim and Ismail agreed. But as Ibrahim was about to sacrifice his son, *Allah* switched Ismail with a Ram (male goat) at the last moment. Hence, on this day, Muslims offer sacrifices of a goat, sheep or camel all over the world. Though in India, it is usually goat. The festival also marks the completion of Hajj (pilgrimage to Mecca, Saudi Arabia).

HOLI

The festival of colours or Holi welcomes the bright and colourful spring season. It is a full moon day and is celebrated in the month of Phalgun (February-March) of the **Hindu lunar calendar**. A fun filled festival for people of all ages, Holi is when houses get their spring cleaning, sweets fill the markets and people paint colours on each other.

On the first day, bonfires are lit at night to signify burning the demoness **Holika**, Hiranyakashipu's sister. It is said that the demon-king Hiranyakashipu's son **Prahlad** was an ardent follower of Lord Vishnu. This upset his father, who wanted everyone to worship him and think of him as God. Prahlad ignored his father's wishes and continued worshipping Vishnu. This enraged the king and he decided to kill his own son. Hiranyakashipu ordered his sister, Holika to carry Prahlad in her arms and walk into burning flames as Holika would be saved because of her boon from the God of flames. Even though it was Prahlad who was to be inflamed, exactly the opposite happened. Lord Vishnu saved the lad and Holika died. Hiranyakashipu did not know that for one hour, the boon of protection from the flames did not work and he had unknowingly chosen that exact hour. Therefore, Holika died and Prahlad was saved by Lord Vishnu who later took the avatar (form) of Narsingha (half man and half lion) and killed Hiranyakashipu. That is why a night before Holi, bonfires are lit depicting this very tale.

The next day of Holi is 'rang' meaning colour, where people spend the day throwing coloured powder and water at each other. And since no festival is complete without its food, during Holi we eat *gujiya* (a sweet pastry filled with *khoya*), then home made potato chips, rice crisps, papad (papadams) and *chakli* (sweet candy). A special drink called *thandai* is prepared, sometimes containing *bhang* (Cannabis sativa). In the evening of the second day, people visit each others houses and go meet their relatives taking with them good wishes and gifts.

PURIM & PESAH

Purim is a **Jewish** festival celebrated in March, to celebrate the escape of the Jews from the clutches of the Persian king. It is believed that the king wanted to kill all the Jews, but his wife, the Queen was a Jew herself and saved her people even at the cost of her own life. On this day, the story of how the Jews escaped is read. In the evening, the whole family gets together for a feast. Gifts are exchanged, charity is also distributed. It is customary to give at least two poor people some sort of monetary help on this day.

Purim is followed by another important Jewish festival called the Pesah or Passover. It is celebrated in April, over a period of eight days. This festival marks the 'passing over' or sparing of the Jews by the Angel of Death in 1250 BC. It is said that when the Jewish families wanted to leave Egypt, to escape the massacre by the then Pharoah, the Angel of Death passed over the Jewish households, sparing the Jewish children. The next day when the Pharaoh let the Jews leave Egypt, they fled with Moses leading the way and reached the Promised Land, now known as Israel.

BHAI DOOJ

This festival comes twice a year - once after Holi and the other time after Diwali. The name itself denotes the meaning of the festival. It falls on *dooj*, the second day after the full moon. The festival is celebrated between brothers and sisters to strengthen the bond of love they share. On this auspicious day, sisters put *tilak* or *teeka* on their brother's forehead and pray for their long life. In return, brothers pamper their sisters and promise them to stand by their side in all hardships of life.

"It is believed that once Yamraj (the god of death) visited his sister Yami. His sister became very delighted to see him and applied a *tilak* on his forehead. At this, Yamraj became so happy that he announced that the person whose sister will apply tilak on his forehead on that day would become free from the fear of death and hell. From that day, the tradition of *Bhai Dooj* came into existence.

"Another mythological tale says that after killing the devil, Narkasur, lord Krishna went to his sister Subhadra. The day on which lord Krishna visited his sister was the second day after the new-moon day, or the *dooj* day. Subhadra gave her brother a warm welcome by doing his *arti*, applying a *tilak* on his forehead, sprinkling flowers over him, and offering him sweets. From then onwards, it became a tradition and got fame as the *Bhai Dooj* festival.

RAMA NAVAMI

Celebrated in the month of April, Rama Navami is the birthday of the Hindu God Rama. The festival commemorates the birth of Rama who is remembered for his prosperous and righteous reign. People normally perform Kalyanotsavam (marriage celebration) for small idols of Rama and Sita in their houses, and at the end of the day the deity is taken to a procession on the streets.

For the occasion, Hindus are supposed to fast (or restrict themselves to a specific diet). Temples are decorated and readings of the Ramayana take place. Along with Shri Rama, people also pray to Sita (Rama's wife), Lakshmana (his brother who went on exile with him) and Hanuman (monkey God, ardent devotee of Rama and Rama's chief of army).

In Ayodhya, the birth place of Rama, this festival is celebrated with a special joy.

MAHAVIR JAYANTI

Mahavir Jayanti is celebrated to honour the birthday of **Lord Mahavir**, the founder of the **Jain religion**. It falls usually during March/April. On Mahavir Jayanti, Jain temples are decorated with flags. In the morning the idol of Mahavira is given a ceremonial bath called the 'abhishek'. It is then placed in a cradle and carried in a procession around the neighbourhood. The devotees make offerings of milk, rice, fruit, incense, lamps and water to the people in procession. This festival is celebrated by all Jains in the world and is a big day for them.

BAISAKHI

Celebrated on the 13th of April each year, Baisakhi is one of the main festivals of the **Sikhs**.

It commemorates the establishment of the Khalsa in 1699, which marks the Sikh New Year. Besides Punjab, Baisakhi is widely celebrated as a harvest festival in other northern states of India, such as Haryana, Himachal Pradesh and Uttaranchal.

On Baisakhi people flock to the Gurudwaras and listen to the recitations of the Guru Granth Sahib. The Golden Temple in Amritsar draws huge crowds on this day.

It also is observed as the beginning of the New Year by Indians in West Bengal, Kerala, and some other regions of India. In Kerala, the festival is called Vishu. In Andhra Pradesh, it is Ugadi or the new beginning. In Bengal, it is known as Naba Barsha meaning New Year. In Manipur it is known as Lai Haraoba when people sing and dance. Assamese celebrate the festival as Bohag Bihu while in Maharashtra it is known as the Gudi Padva.

EASTER

Easter is celebrated on the Sunday after the full moon in the month of April. It recalls the Resurrection of Jesus Christ and is a day of great joy for Christians. It is believed that after three days of his crucifixion, a miracle occurred and Jesus returned from the dead. The day Lord Jesus died on the cross is called Good Friday. It is a day for mourning, sermons, prayers and fast. It is believed that since Lord Christ died for the good of mankind, this day is particularly holy and is named Good Friday. After three days comes Easter Sunday, a festival of joy on Christ's return. People exchange cards and Easter eggs, that being a symbol of Jesus' return and new life to Christians. The humble egg assumes importance on Easter as it symbolizes new beginning. The Easter Bunny symbolizes the coming of spring and life.

BUDDHA PURNIMA

The birth anniversary of Buddha is celebrated as Buddha Purnima. It falls on the full moon day in the month of Baisakh (April-May). Considered a very holy day for the Buddhists, they bathe and wear white clothes on Buddha Purnima/Jayanti and offer prayers in their monasteries or places of worship. Special attention is paid to peepal trees because it was under a peepal tree that Buddha gained enlightenment. Diyas and lamps are lit around the trees and the trees are decorated with flowers. Devotees also place bright flags and place fruits under the trees. As a symbol of freedom, caged birds are also freed on this day. Celebrations are very festive in Bodhgaya in Bihar and in Sarnath in Uttar Pradesh. Places like Arunachal Pradesh, Sikkim and Ladakh, where there is a large Buddhist population, also celebrate this festival with zest. Another important Buddhist celebration is the Kaza Festival of Ladakh held in the month of June. Here the Dalai Lama is worshipped as the living incarnation of Lord Buddha. People do a mask dance on this day to frighten away evil spirits.

PATETI

Pateti is a Parsi festival which marks the beginning of the New Year for the Parsis, followers of Zoroastrianism. The majority of the Parsis wear traditional new clothes consisting of sacred vests, gara sarees, duglees and ornaments. Then the Parsi family goes to the fire temple of the agiary. People pray and repent over all their sins. They offer milk, flowers, water, fruits, and even sandalwood to the sacred fire. The house is also decorated with flowers and rangolis, in which a motif of a fish is used.

The day on which Pateti falls is noteworthy because it falls on the spring equinox, that is, the day and night are of equal duration and both the North Pole and the South Pole have sunlight.

Another important day for the Parsis is **Khordad Sal**. It is the birthday of the prophet Zoroaster. Khordad Sal comes six days after Pateti. On this day, special prayers and discourses are held in the agiary on good deeds, thoughts and charity.

RATH YATRA

Rath Yatra is not a festival of the home, it is a community affair. Rath Yatra means a chariot ride. This event is in the honour of Lord Jagannath, another name of Lord Krishna. It is celebrated especially in the state of Orissa in the month of Aashadh (June-July). Even though this festival is celebrated in other places too, the main Rath Yatra takes place in the holy Town of Puri at Orissa. Lacs of people visit Puri to witness this experience! In the

Jagannath temple, Lord Krishna, his elder brother Balabhadra and their sister Subhadra are worshipped in an unusual trinity. Their images are made of neemwood and are painted in a highly stylized method. According to one legend, Subhadra wanted to visit Dwarka, her parent's home. Therefore her two brothers, Jagannath and Balbhadra took her there on this day. The journey is made on elaborate chariots amidst fervent devotion by lacs of people! Lord Jagannath rides a 14 meter chariot with sixteen wheels and Subhadra rides a twelve meter high, twelve wheeled chariot. Each chariot resembles the temple at Puri. Balabhadra, the eldest brother rides first , followed by Subhadra and then Lord Jagannath. The Journey of the deities in the town of Puri begins at the Jagannath temple and ends at Gunducha Ghar or Lord Jagannath's birthplace now a temple three kilometers away. Thousands of devotees pull the chariots by huge ropes and it is believed that whosoever pulls the chariots achieves moksha or salvation and if somebody unfortunately comes under the wheels, they too experience a life after death full of peace.

TEEJ

It is a festival heralding the onset of the monsoon season in northern India. It symbolizes the coming of the monsoons. It is celebrated with much joy in the states of Rajasthan, Bihar, Uttar Pradesh, Uttaranchal and Delhi. It falls on the third day of the waxing moon in the month of Shravan (July-August).

Teej is a festival for the daughters of the house. It is about celebration of Goddess Parvati's marriage with Lord Shiva. Married women pray to Shiva and Parvati to give them a long, successful married life.

With the first drops of the rain on the parched ground, festivities explode with pomp and show. Women pamper themselves at this time. Hands beautifully designed with *Mehandi* are flashed about. Women follow the tradition of dancing the 'dandiya' dance. Many Teej melas or fairs are also organized all over where stall of bangles, clothes and eatables are very popular.

RAKSHA BANDHAN

Raksha Bandhan represents one of the most sentimental festivals of India. It is based on the emotional ties and bonds a brother and a sister share. It falls on the full moon day in the month of *Shravan* (July-August).

Some popular tales say that once lord Indra was in a war with the demons. The demons seemed to be winning and that was not good news for the Gods. Indra's wife decided to do something about it. She read some scriptures and chanted a holy mantra on a thread. She tied the thread on her husband's wrist telling him it was a 'Raksha Sutra' or protection thread. Indra went on to win the war and defeat the demons!

Another legend says that the Queen of Mewar was being threatened by the mighty army of the Governor Bahadur Shah. He laid a siege around her kingdom. The *Maharani* sent a sacred thread or *rakhi* to the Mughal emperor Humayun. On receiving it, Humayun felt he needed to protect his sister! Humayun came to the queen's rescue and chased Bahadur Shah's army out!

Over the years, *Raksha Bandhan* has become a very popular festival in India. It is celebrated as a festival signifying a loving bond between a brother and a sister.

GANESHA CHATURTHI

Ganesha also known as Ganpati, is the elephant headed Hindu God. He is the son of Shiva and Parvati. Ganesha Chaturthi is the festival celebrated on the fourth day of the Shukla Paksha in the month of Bhadrapad (August-September). It is said that this day Lord Ganesha was born and was declared **first among all the Gods**. For Hindus, this day is very important as they consider Ganesha to be the remover of all obstacles and the bestower of good fortune. In India, this festival is celebrated with great fervour in the state of Maharashta, where it is also called Vinayak Chaturthi.

Who is Ganapati and what is Ganesh Chaturthi?

Ganesha also known as Ganapati, is the elephant-headed Hindu God. He is the son of Shiva and Parvati.

Legends say that Parvati created a beautiful boy from the dirt of her body, treated him as her son and gave him the responsibility of guarding her home. Shiva, her husband, did not know about this and when he came home he was confronted and challenged by the 'boy' created by his wife Parvati. The boy refused to let Shiva into his own home! Shiva became very angry and a clash ensued. The fall out was that Shiva chopped the boy's head off! When Parvati got to know of this, she was very angry with Shiva and later burst into tears. Seeing Parvati's condition, Shiva was filled with guilt and remorse at his wrong doing. He immediately sent his soldiers to the forest to bring the head of the first being they see sleeping facing north. The soldiers came across an elephant. Thus, an elephant head was brought and placed on the life less boy. With his new elephant head, the boy came alive and he became Ganesha or the elephant headed one! Ganesha is regarded by one and all, as the remover of obstacles, and he should be offered worship first, before any form of worship is offered to any other Gods.

JANAMASTHAMI

Krishna is the eighth of the ten incarnations of Lord Vishnu, the Preserver of the Universe. All through his childhood, Krishna performed amazing miracles. Janamasthami is a festival celebrating the **birth of Lord Krishna**. Janam means 'birth' and Ashtami means 'eighth day'. Since the day falls on the eighth day of the lunar fortnight, so his birthday is called Janamasthami. It occurs on the eighth day of the Krishna Paksha in the month of Bhadrapad (August-September). It is celebrated with great fervour and gaiety in the states of Uttar Pradesh, Maharashtra and other northern states.

Devotees fast, temples are decorated and an idol of his baby form is kept in a cradle and the devotees take turn pulling its string to rock the baby Krishna. At the stroke of twelve bells chime, conches blow and loud sounds of 'Hare Krishna' fill the air. This is to announce the birth of the Lord. Sweets prepared from milk and curd are eaten.

As a child Krishna loved milk and curd and earlier in the day, a game called 'dahi handi' was played. Even today, this game continues where people make a human pyramid to climb up to a height where the 'handi' is hung. When the human pyramid is being built, the others splash water and in jest taunt the climbers, trying to make their task as difficult as possible. This way, the victory of good over evil is celebrated exuberantly in this colourful and vibrant festival.

ONAM

Kerala was once home to the **king Mahabali**, who was the grandson of Prahlad and son of Valchana, both great kings. Onam is celebrated for three days in memory of that time, the golden age of Kerala. The people believe that Mahabali comes to Kerala to see his people once in a year because of a boon granted to him by Lord Vishnu in his Vaman avatar. This festival is celebrated on the twelfth day of the waning moon in the month of Bhadrapad (August-September). The festival is the harbinger of spring - signaling the start of the harvest season. Onam epitomizes the newfound vigour and enthusiasm of the season, and is celebrated with traditional fervour with visits to temples, family get-togethers, gifting of clothes called Onakkodi and lots of merrymaking. To welcome their king, Kerala comes alive during Onam. Homes are decorated with fresh flowers. King Mahabali is welcomed with 'pookalam' or flower mat, which is a must for every home. Everyone in the family buys new clothes and scrumptious sweets and great vegetarian dishes are served on banana leaves. For entertainment, the popular Indian dance, 'Kathakali' is staged and finally 'Vallamkali' or the boat race takes place as one of the main attractions of Onam. This is where over a hundred oarsmen row together and sing the song of the boatman in chorus.

NAVRATRI & DURGA PUJA

'Navratri' are nine auspicious days which are celebrated as the days of **Goddess Durga**. This festival occurs twice a year, at the change from winter to summer in the spring, and again at the change from summer to winter in the autumn. The autumn festival is celebrated from the first day of the ninth day of Ashwin (September - October), while the Spring festival is celebrated in Chaitra (April-May). The two Navratri celebrations are known as Ram-Navratri in Chaitra and Durga Navratri in Ashwin.

Goddess Durga is worshipped in nine different forms. One sees her as Goddess Lakshmi for peace and prosperity and the other as Goddess Saraswati, as the Goddess of knowledge. It is believed that on this day, Goddess Durga killed the demon Mahishasura and rid the world of his evils.

In northern India, a dry coconut is covered with red cloth and placed on a small pot in the *puja ghar*, symbolizing the Goddess. Then, a few *jowar* seeds are planted in a pot and kept near it. Generally, the ladies of the house fast for the nine days and consume only special Navratra food. On the eighth or the ninth day i.e. Ashtami or Navami, they make *suji halwa*, *puris* and *chanas* for *Prasad*. They feed seven or nine young unmarried girls as the Goddess Durga is also worshiped in the form of a kanya or girl.

In Bengal, this is called 'Durga Puja'. Day and night celebrations take place as this is a time for complete family festivity. During Durga Puja, beautiful idols of the Mother Goddess are worshipped on grand stages or *pandals* (temporary structures set up to venerate the goddess) for those nine days. On the ninth day, the idols are transported out in a procession to be immersed in a river or pond.

DUSSEHRA

It falls on the tenth day of the waxing moon in the month of Ashwin (September - October). This festival celebrates the victory of **Lord Rama**, the prince of Ayodhya, over the mighty ruler of Lanka, the ten-headed demon king **Ravan**, who had abducted Rama's wife Sita and taken her to his kingdom of Lanka.

Dussehra is also called as Vijaydashmi as it celebrates the victory of good over evil. Dussehra or Dasha-hara means 'victory over the ten-faced one.'

KARVA CHAUTH

Nine days before Diwali, the festival of Karva Chauth is celebrated. This festival is mainly celebrated in Punjab, Rajasthan, Uttar Pradesh and Gujarat but other states follow this belief as well. Women pray to the Moon God asking for the well being and long life of their husbands. For this they keep a fast and only break it on sighting the moon.

DEEPAVALI

In Hindi, 'Deepavali' literally means a 'row of lamps' and Diwali as it is popularly known, means the 'festival of light'. We celebrate Diwali in the month of Kartik (October - November) on the darkest moonless night or Amavasya. It is the main festival of many Hindus and is celebrated with lights, crackers, sweets, and feasts throughout India. Prayers are ordered to invoke the Goddess Lakhmi, the Hindu Goddess of Wealth. It marks the coming of winters and the beginning of the New Year especially for the people in Gujarat. The festival actually starts from the thirteenth day of the waning moon or the second day of the waxing moon.

There are five days of Diwali, each day with a special significance. The first day is called 'Dhanteras' which is important for the business community of India. 'Dhan' means wealth and 'teras' means the thirteenth day of the Hindu month. This day is also considered auspicious because it is the birthday of the Lord Dhanwantari. Another noteworthy reason for this day is the God Yama or the God of Death is worshipped to provide prosperity and well being to people.

The second day of Diwali is called Naraka Chaturdashi or chhoti Diwali. The legend goes that on this day Lord Krishna destroyed the demon Nakasura and made the world free from his terror. Nakasura was the son of the Goddess Earth and had a demonic bent of mind. The third day is the actual Diwali. it is on this day that Lord Rama, Lord Vishnu's seventh incarnation returned to the city of Ayodhya with his wife Sita, after killing the Lankan ruler Ravan.

It is also an important day because this is the only day when Goddess Lakshmi comes down to earth. People perform Lakshmi Puja (worship of Goddess Lakshmi) on Diwlali, seeking wealth and prosperity for the whole year.

The day after the Diwali is known as Annakoot. On this day Govardhan mountain or the mountain of food is worshipped. According to legend, Lord Krishna had asked the people of his village to stop worshipping Lord Indra. When Indra heard about this he was enraged and therefore lashed out on the village through a rain storm which continued for seven days. In order to protect his village, Lord Krishna picked up the entire Govardhan Mountain and held it on his little finger while the entire village was under it like an umbrella. Thus, this day after Diwali is celebrated as Govardhan Puja.

The fifth and final day of Diwali Festival is known as Bhai Dooj. This day is observed as a symbol of love between sisters and brothers.

CHHATPUJA

Chhat Puja is an important festival in eastern India, especially in the state of Bihar. It comes six days after Deepavali. This festival is basically a thanks giving to the Sun God, Surya! The duration of this festival is two days and is usually celebrated in the month of Kartik (October-November).

On the first day, a fast is kept. Before the fast, devotees have a bath or holy cleansing. The fast is broken in the evening after a family prayer session in front of the temple at home. Seasonal fruits and special delicacies are offered as 'prasaad'. These are shared amongst all family members.

On the second day, devotees actually camp on the banks of the river. The day starts with a twenty-four hour fast. The women of the house spruce up their kitchens squeaky clean and make a 'prasad' to offer the divine Sun God.

The freshly harvested crop of wheat and rice becomes the main ingredients in the prasaad. The sweet meats prepared as offerings are supposed to be the favourites of Lord Surya so the cooking is done with strict supervision. The lady in charge, abstains from wearing clothes that are stitched and refuses to eat cooked meals. No one can enter this kitchen without a bath.

Men folk sit outside the house on guard. Later, they guard the baskets of prasaad at the riverside. The women folk carry six baskets containing food, flowers and clay elephants as an offering to the Sun God, to the nearest river or lake. Hands holding the basket are held up so as to not contaminate the offering by touch. Then, they stand in the water for many hours chanting mantras and paying obeisance to lord Surya. They keep on standing in water, be it a cold day or hot and the offerings remain immersed in water. Some women undertake even harder vows if their wishes are fulfilled. There is no priest to conduct the ceremony. After immersion, the food is considered blessed and then the women who had been starving, consume it first as the prasaad of lord Surya. Later it is distributed to everyone. Large fairs are also organized along the river front, with different stalls of food and entertainment. This festival fosters the spirit of community worship, sharing and perseverance.

GURUPURAB

Gurupurab is one of the most important Sikh festivals. The Sikhs celebrate ten Gurupurabs in a year. Each marks either the birth, death or martyrdom days of the Sikh Gurus. The most significant Gurupurab is that of the birth anniversary of the first Sikh Guru, Guru Nanak. It is also called Guru Nanak Jayanti and is celebrated in the month of Kartiki (November).

Fifteen days before Gurunanak Jayanti, the uninterrupted reading of the holy book of the Sikhs, the 'Guru Granth Sahib' also begins. This is called Akand Path. It concludes on the day of Guru Nanak Jayaanti.

ID-UL-FITR

It is the most auspicious festival for Muslims all over the world. The festival of Id-ul-Fitr marks the culmination of the holy month of Ramzan. It is celebrated on the first day of the next month, namely Shawwal, which starts when three people sight the new moon. Id-ul-Fitr marks the end of the month of fasting of *Roza*. It literally means breaking of fast. It is the third 'pillar' or religious obligation of Islam and also a way of coming closer to Allah. Each year, during the month of Ramzan, from sunrise to sunset, Muslims abstain from

food and drink in a form of self-purification. They do not even drink water during the daytime. Praying, offering *namaz* and reading the *Quran* are the traditional rituals during *roza*. After the sunset, the fast or *roza* is broken with fruits and food. Pious Muslims believe that during Ramzan, the doors to paradise or *Jannat* are open and those of hell are closed. Those who fast believe that they will be forgiven for their sins and will be permitted to go to *Jannat*. On Id-ul-Fitr greetings of 'Id Mubarak' or 'blessed Eid' ring all around as people meet and greet each other. Muslims celebrate not only the end of fasting but also thank God for the self control and strength that Muslims believe God gave them. It is a time of giving and sharing, and many Muslims dress in holiday attire.

Christmas Day. It is celebrated on the **25th of December** as the birthday of Lord Jesus Christ. Special prayers or a mass is held in the church for Christ.

The celebrations for Christmas start from Christmas Eve, i.e. the twenty fourth of December. People go for Midnight Mass, sing hymns and carols in church. Churches are decorated with flowers, and lit with candles for the Christmas Evening. The priest gives a sermon in which the message would be of love and salvation. People gather in good numbers to pray and thank God for his sacrifices that are believed to have saved mankind.

Modern customs of the holiday include gift-giving, church celebrations, and the display of various decorations-including the Christmas tree, lights, mistletoe, nativity scenes and holly. The jolly mythological figure Santa Claus, or Father Christmas, is also a major aspect of Christmas. He is traditionally believed by millions of children as being a bringer of gifts on or before Christmas Day.

With only six more days left for the New Year to begin, following Christmas people wish each other, "Merry Christmas and a Happy New Year." Fun, frolic and laughter mark this year-end festival.

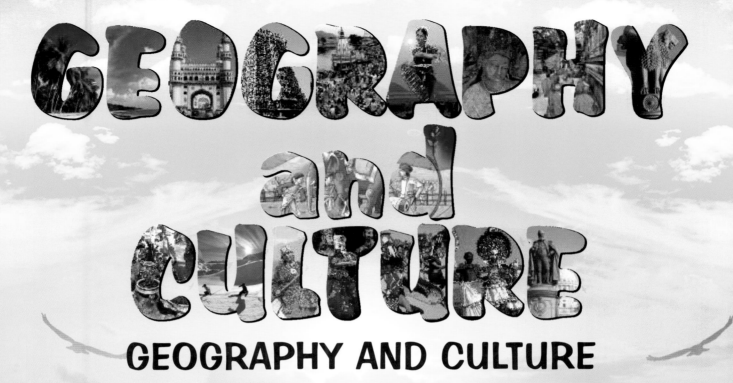

GEOGRAPHY AND CULTURE

India, the seventh largest country in the world is well marked off from the rest of Asia by mountains and the sea, which gives the country a distinct geographical entity. It covers an area of 32,87,2631 square kilometers. Lying entirely in the northern hemisphere the mainland extends 3214 km from north to south between extreme latitudes and about 2933 km from east to west between extreme longitudes. It has a land frontier of about 15200 km.

The country is surrounded by the Bay of Bengal in the east, the Arabian Sea in the west and the Indian Ocean to the south. The total length of the coastline of the mainland, Lakshwadeep group of islands and Andaman and Nicobar group of islands is 7,516.5 km

PHYSICAL FEATURES

The Indian sub-continent is characterized by great diversity in its physical features. It may be divided into following physical units:

Himalayan Mountains

Himalayas, the highest mountain system in the world, is also one of the world's youngest mountain ranges. It extends practically uninterrupted for a distance of some 2500 km and covers an area of about 500,000 sq km. It contains the world's highest mountain peak, Mt. Everest, and some ten peaks rising above 7,500 m. Kanchanjunga (8598 Mtrs) is the highest mountain peak in India. The Greater Himalayas which have an average altitude of 6000 m have within them almost all the prominent peaks such Everest (8848m), Kanchenjunga (8598m) Nanga Parbat (8126m), Nanda Devi (7817m) and Namcha Parbat (7756m).

The Indus-Gangetic Plain

The Indo-Gangetic Plain lies in between the Himalayas and the southern peninsula which includes the valley of Bhramputra, the Ganges and the Indus river and their branches. The eternal city of Varanasi; the beautiful Sunderbans; the splendid Taj Mahal and the charming Khajuraho temples fall in this region.

Peninsular Plateau

Rising from the alluvial plains of Uttar Pradesh and Bihar, south of the Yamuna Ganga line, the great Indian plateau extends towards the south to encompass the whole of Peninsula. The Peninsula is flanked on one

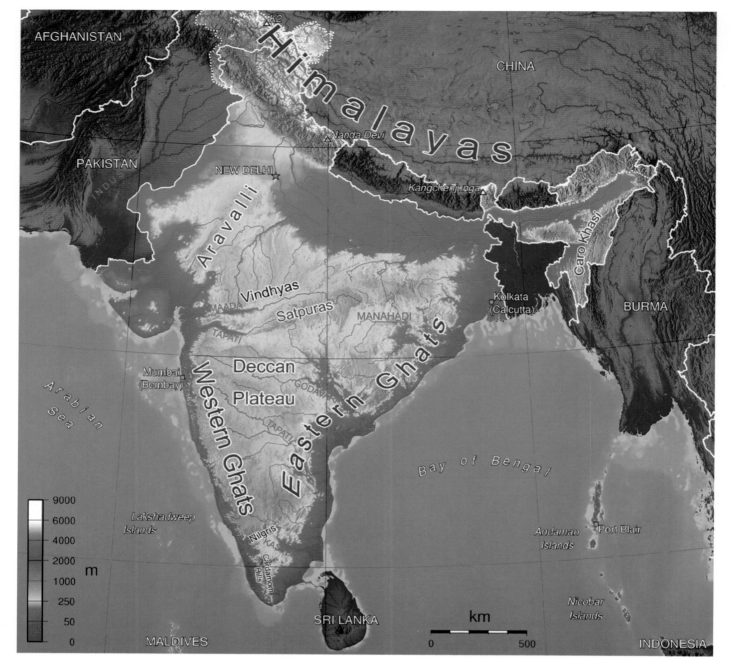

side by the Eastern Ghats and on the other by the Western Ghats. The southern point of plateau is formed by the Nilgiri Hills where the Eastern and the Western Ghats meet. The Cardamom Hills lying beyond may be regarded as a continuation of the Western Ghats.

The Desert region

The desert region can be divided into two parts - the great desert and the little desert. The great desert extends from the edge of the Rann of Kuchch beyond the Luni River northward. The whole of the Rajasthan-Sind frontier runs through this. The little desert extends from the Luni between Jaisalmer and Jodhpur up to the northern wastes. Between the great and the little deserts lies a zone of absolute sterile country, consisting of rocky land cut up by limestone ridges.

STATES AND CULTURE

India is home to 28 states and 7 union territories. Every state has its own distinct culture, cuisine, language and monument that give it its character. The 28 states are described below with their distinct characteristics.

ANDHRA PRADESH

Known as the 'Rice Bowl of India', Andhra Pradesh is a state in southern India. India's third largest state, Andhra Pradesh's regional and official language is **Telegu** while its capital is **Hyderabad**. Hyderabad is essentially a modern city, which combined with Secunderabad is known as the twin cities and is among the seven largest cities in India.

You'll find the spiciest food in Andhra Pradesh, known to the spiciest of all Indian cuisine. Hyderabadi cuisine is influenced by the Muslims who arrived in Telangana in the 14th century. Much of the cuisine revolves around meat like lamb, chicken and fish. It is rich and aromatic, with a liberal use of exotic spices and ghee. The **biryani** is perhaps the most distinctive and popular of Hyderabadi dishes.

Kuchipudi is the state's best-known classical dance form of Andhra Pradesh. It is essentially a narrative dance enunciation of Puranic legends.

One of the early generals, Salar Jung, was noted for his voluminous collections of antiques and rare art treasures which were housed in a showpiece landmark of Hyderabad, the Salar Jung Museum, now given the status of a National Museum.

Andhra Pradesh is the state with the most cinema halls in India, at around 3000. The state producing about 200 movies a year, is also the largest movie industry in India.

Landmarks

The famed **Charminar** built in the end of the 16th century is one of the landmarks of Hyderabad. It rises to four stories and has space for a mosque on its topmost floor. It is these four (char) minarets (minar) that give the building, its name 'Charminar'. Called the 'Arc De Triumph of the East', Charminar symbolises Hyderabad. Adjacent to the Charminar is the impressive Mecca Mosque, reputed to be among the largest in the world.

Tirupati or Tirumala is a very important pilgrimage for Hindus throughout India. It is the richest holy temple city in India. Its main temple is dedicated to the god Tirupati. One monument not to be missed is the 400-year-old majestic and imposing **Golconda** Fort. Considered one of India's most outstanding citadels, the Golconda fort epitomises the sumptuous 'Nawabi' culture of the time. It has an interesting story behind it. One day, a shepherd boy came across an idol on the rocky hill, which was called Mangalavaram. The news was conveyed to the ruling Kakatiya king. The king got a mud fort constructed around the holy spot and his descendents continued to follow this trend.

DID YOU KNOW?
Golconda gave the world some of the best-known diamonds, including the 'Kohinoor' or 'Mountain of Light'. It passed through many hands but eventually ended up with the East India Company Treasury. It is now a part of the British Crown Jewels.

ARUNACHAL PRADESH

To the north of Assam lies Arunachal Pradesh. With its capital as **Itangar**, it has many principal languages including **Monpa**, **Miji**, **Tangsa** and **Wancho**. Much of the State is covered by the Himalayas. Arunachal Pradesh means 'land of the dawn lit mountains' and is also known as 'land of the rising sun'.

At Tawang at an altitude of 10,000 feet is India's largest Buddhist monastery, where the 6th Dalai Lama was born. Tawang Monastery or Gompa also known as the 'Galden Namgyal Lhatse' is a 400 year old Buddhist monastery of the Mahayana sect, built in the 17th century. There is a towering 18 ft high gilded statue of the Buddha in the monastery complex.

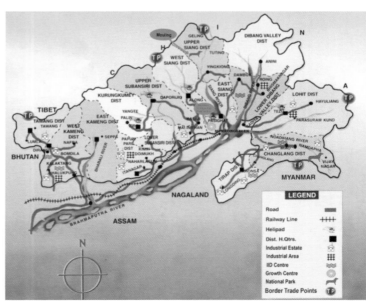

ASSAM

The word 'Assam' is probably derived from the Sanskrit word Asoma meaning peerless or unparalleled. Its capital is **Dispur** and the principal language spoken **Assamese**.

It is also known as 'The Land of the Red River and the Blue Hills' - the red river is the Brahmaputra River and the blue hills are the hills surrounding the river valley. Assam is known for her rich forest wealth which constitutes 22.21 per cent of the total forest area.

Bihu is particular to this state and is the chief festival celebrated on three occasions of the year. Assam is also famous for its **tea plantation** and its tea is devoured throughout the country. More than half of India's tea is grown in Assam. Paat and muga are two types of silk that come from Assam. They are considered some of the finest silks in the world.

The State has five National Parks and eleven wildlife sanctuaries. The Kaziranga National Park and the Manas Tiger Project (National Park) are internationally famous for one horned Rhino and Royal Bengal Tiger respectively.

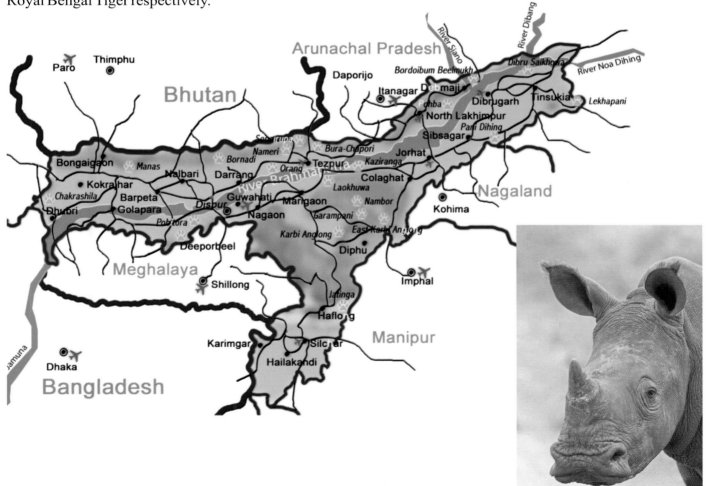

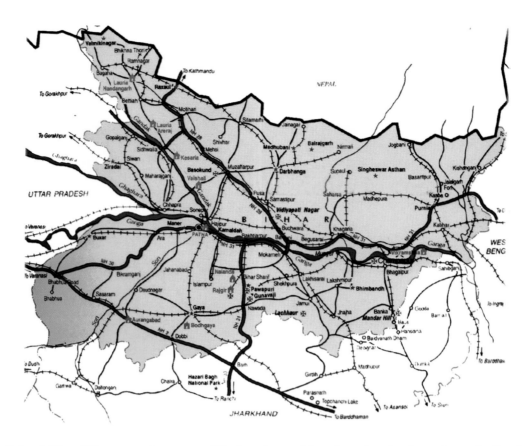

BIHAR

Bihar is a part of the 150 million people strong Bhojpuri speaking heartland of northern India. Its capital is **Patna** and the principal language spoken is **Hindi** along with **Angika**, **Bhojpuri**, **Magahi** and **Maithili**. The name Bihar is derived from the Sanskrit Vihara, meaning "abode". At one time, Viharas filled the large countryside and cities of Bihar.

Bihar is most famous for its status as the birthplace of iconic global and Indian symbols like Buddhism, the 10th Guru of the Sikhs-Guru Gobind Singh, the Indian Rupee, and ancient Bihari Imperial symbols like the Maurya Lions and Ashok Chakra. Symbolically, the first President of India, Dr. Rajendra Prasad, was a Bihari. The capital city of Patna was once known as Patliputra, home to a string of Indian monarchs that ruled over much of the Indian-subcontinent and had an empire that reached as far as Iran.

Chhath, also called Dala Chhath - is an ancient and major festival in Bihar, and is celebrated twice a year. Bihar is also famous for its robust cinema industry in the Bhojpuri language.

Landmarks

If one visits Bihar they should not miss out on the **Mahabodhi Temple Complex** at Bodh Gaya, which is located in the central part of the state. It is the part of the great Ganges plains. Bihar is one of the four holy sites related to the life of the Lord Buddha, and the Mahabodhi Temple is situated at the place of Lord Buddha's enlightenment.

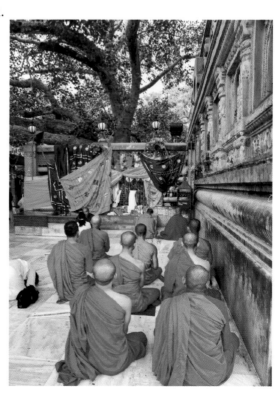

The first temple was built by Emperor Ashoka in the 3rd century BC, and the present temple dates from the 5th or 6th centuries. It is one of the earliest Buddhist temples built entirely with brick, still standing in India, from the late Gupta period. Along the western wall of the temple is the 'bodhi tree'. Under this tree is the Vajrasana, the Diamond Throne, a stone slab marking the site where the Buddha was sitting when he attained enlightenment.

CHHATTISGARH

Chattisgarh considers itself a true 21st Century state and received statehood on November 1, 2000 after being carved out of Madhya Pradesh. With its capital as **Raipur**, the principal language of this state is **Hindi** and **Chattisgarhi**. It is also the 10th largest state of India by area.

Almost half of the state (44%) is covered in forests, an obvious reason for the common nickname of 'The Green State'. Chhattisgarh takes its name from 36 (Chattis is thirty-six in Hindi and Garh is Fort) princely states in this region from very old times.

Chitrakote Falls, a spot where the river Indravati has an abrupt fall of 96 ft, which are like horse shoe curve, are often compared to the Niagara Falls.

GOA

Located on the west coast of India, Goa is India's smallest state in terms of area and the fourth smallest in terms of population. The state's luscious forests and beautiful landscape has inspired many natives to call it 'the emerald land'.

The name Goa is said to have been derived from the Konkani word 'Goy', which means a patch of tall grass. The Indian epic Mahabharata refers to the area now known as Goa, as 'Goparashtra' or 'Govarashtra' which means a nation of cowherds. Goa is sometimes referred to as "The Pearl of the East."

Following the end of Portuguese rule, the most widely used language is its official language **Konkani** other than **Marathi**. Its capital is **Panaji**.

Landmarks

Ten kilometer east of Panaji, along the Mandovi River in the town of Old Goa, there lies some of India's greatest churches and among them, the most popular and the most revered by Christians worldwide is the **Basilica of Bom Jesus**. The Basilica, dedicated to Infant Jesus, has been declared a World Heritage Monument. 'Bom Jesus' means 'Infant Jesus' or 'Good Jesus'. Renowned throughout the Catholic world, the 16th century cathedral is India's first Minor Basilica, and is considered as one of the best examples of baroque architecture in India.

GUJARAT

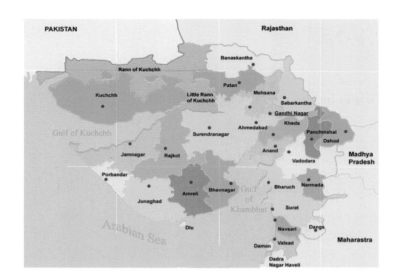

A state in western India, Gujarat according to historians gets its name from the Prakrit Guijar Ratta or Guijar Rashtra (meaning land of the Guijars). The Guijars were an ancient tribe of India that wandered through present day Punjab and Rajasthan before settling in western India.

Its capital is **Gandhinagar** and the principal language spoken is **Gujarati**. Full of great cultural and national pride, Gujaratis often refer to their home state as the Land of Krishna and Gandhi.

Every year on January 14th, Ahmedabad in Gujarat hosts the **International Kite Festival**. Two famous dances originating from Gujarat are the **Dandiya Raas** and the **Garba**. The roots of Dandiya Raas are laid from the days of Lord Krishna who played raas on the shores of Yamuna River on a moonlit night with his beloved Gopis. Whereas Garba is a very graceful form of dance mainly performed by females in a circular formation, it is in reverences of goddess Ambaji.

Like Bhojpuri Cinema of Bihar, Gujarat also has its own Gujarati cinema which completed 75 years in 2007. Gujarati film started its journey in 1922 and from mythology to history, social to political, Gujarati cinema has experimented with such stories and issues all these years.

Landmarks

The **Sun Temple** at Modhera is one of the finest examples of Indian temple architecture. The temple dedicated to the Sun God or Surya, stands on a plinth overlooking a deep stone-stepped tank. Every inch of the edifice is carved with figures of Gods, animals and flowers.

Another place to visit is in **Bhuj town** and is called the Aina Mahal (The Mirror Palace). It has walls of marble covered with mirrors separated by gilded ornaments with shades of Venetian glass.

The State is also the proud custodian of the Gir Forest National Park. This wildlife sanctuary is the sole home of the pure Asiatic Lions. The area is considered one of the most important protected areas in Asia due to its supported species.

HARYANA

Carved out of the state of Punjab in 1966, the state of Haryana has the second highest per capita income in the country and is considered the current growth engine of India. It is also one of the leading industrialized states of India. Gurgaon, one of the major cities in Haryana is known for its software and BPO centres.

Haryana shares its capital **Chandigarh** with the state of Punjab. Its principal language is **Hindi**, although **Haryanvi** is also spoken locally. The name Haryana itself means 'The Abode of God' from Hari (the Hindu God Vishnu) and ayana (home).

Landmarks

The **Surajkund Crafts Mela** of International fame is held every year in the month of February by Haryana Tourism. This Mela (Fair) highlights some of the finest handloom and handicraft traditions of India. Each year there is a different 'theme state' whose handicrafts are more prominently showcased. Folk theater and music are also featured. Beyond Surajkund is the **Badhkal Lake** with a rest house overlooking its stretch of water. A few miles southwards is the Sultanpur Bird Sanctuary, and further, the hot spring of Sohna.

There are several Mughal monuments in Haryana of which the most popular is **Pinjore Gardens** at the base of the Shivalik hills on the road to Shimla. One interesting fact about Haryana is that every February the town of Sohna hosts India's Annual Vintage Car Rally.

HIMACHAL PRADESH

Himachal Pradesh situated in the heart of the Western Himalya, is identified as 'Dev Bhumi' and is believed to be the abode of God and Goddesses. The literal meaning of Himachal Pradesh is 'Land of snowy mountains'.

With its capital as **Shimla**, the principal language of the state is **Hindi** and **Pahari**. It has one of the highest per capita incomes of any state in India. Due to the abundance of perennial rivers, Himachal also sells hydro electricity to other states such as Delhi, Punjab and Rajasthan. The economy of the state is highly dependent upon three sources i.e. Hydel power, tourism & agriculture.

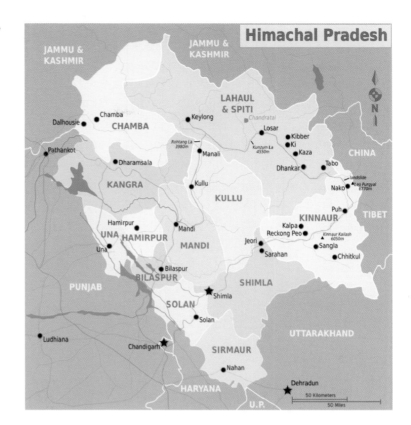

Landmarks

Shimla, the state capital is home to Asia's only natural Ice skating rink. **Naati** is the most popular folk dance of the State. Narkanda at a height of 8,850 feet and 64 kilometers from Shimla on the Hindustan-Tibet road is famous for its apple orchards and its beautiful scenery. These apples are grown and exported to the other states.

Kulu Valley on the banks of the Beas is famous for its apple orchards, its old wooden temples and its folk music and dances. When discussing the valley of Kullu, Rudyard Kipling wrote "Surely the Gods live here; there is no place for men." Kangra is one of the most beautiful and charming valleys in the Himalaya. Dharmashala, the headquarters of the Kangra district is located at the foot of the Dhauladhar Range. This is where His Holiness, the Dalai Lama, now lives.

JAMMU & KASHMIR

The Kashmir valley, often known as paradise on Earth, is famous for its beautiful mountainous landscape while Jammu's numerous holy shrines attract tens of thousands of Hindu and Muslim pilgrims every year.

Jammu and Kashmir often referred to as J&K has two capitals, one for the summer and the other for winter, where **Srinagar** is the Summer Capital and **Jammu** is the winter capital. The principal languages spoken are Kashmiri, Dogri, Gujri, Punjabi, Urdu, Dalti, Dadri, Pahari and Ladakhi.

Within J&K, **Ladakh**, also known as 'Little Tibet', is renowned for its remote mountain beauty and Buddhist culture. Handicrafts are the traditional industry of the State and products like shawls, furniture and other materials are well known throughout India.

Landmarks

By far the most important shrine to North India's Hindus is the cave temple of **Vaishno Devi**, located 60 kilometers north-west of Jammu city. Thousands of devotees make this pilgrimage yearly.

In Srinagar, the **Dal Lake** is a beautiful spot to visit and can be explored in the almost decadent comfort of the Shikaras or hand-paddled water taxis. The famous Boulevard road circles the Dal Lake and leads towards the magnificent Mughal Gardens. The first two gardens - Chashma Shahi and Pari Mahal are to the right of the Boulevard while the other two larger gardens - Nishat and Shalimar are located much further down the Boulevard.

The white marble mosque of Hazratbal is a sacred spot for Muslims. It possesses a hair of Prophet Mohammed. Foremost among the mosques in the valley is the Jami Masjid, a massive congregational mosque.

Pahalgam, **Gulmarg** and **Sonamarg** are the three most popular tourist resorts in Kashmir. Pahalgam is popular as it acts as the staging point for the pilgrimage to the sacred iced lingam in the Amarnath Cave. Gulmarg with its famous 18-hole golf course attracts sportsmen in the summer just as its ski runs make it India's premier skiing centre in the winter. Sonamarg, is the smallest of the hill resorts and is located on the road to Ladakh.

Among the most visited monasteries are **Thikse** and **Hemis**. Thikse is a very large monastery built on a triangular spur of a mountain. It is especially noteworthy housing a gigantic seated statue of the Maitreya. Hemis is the richest of the monasteries but the least hospitable. It is famous for its three-day festival which usually takes place in June.

JHARKHAND

Jharkhand came into being on 15 November, 2000, as the 28th State of the Union after being extracted out of Bihar. The name Jharkhand comes from the Sanskrit Jharikhanda which is the ancient name of the regions dense forest - Jharikhanda. The inhabitants are worshipers of Lord Rama.

With its capital as **Ranchi** and its principal language being Hindi, Jharkhand is famed for its mineral wealth and forestry products. The State also has a number of bird sanctuaries and national parks.

Jamshedpur, in Jharkhand is known as the Steel City as it is the property of the Tata Iron and Steel Company. The town has grown around the first steel plant in India by the Parsi industrialist Sir Jamshedji Tata, after whom the city is named.

KARNATAKA

Karnataka is derived from the Kannada words karu and nadu, meaning elevated land. Karu nadu may also be read as Karu (black) and nadu (region), as a reference to the black cotton soil found in the Bayaluseeme region of Karnataka. Its capital is **Bangalore** and the principal language spoken is **Kannada**.

Since the 1980s, Karnataka has emerged as the pan-Indian leader in the field of IT (Information Technology). Karnataka is the manufacturing hub for some of the largest public sector industries in India. Many of India's premier science and technology research centers are also headquartered in Karnataka. It also leads the nation in biotechnology.

Besides being Karnataka's capital, Bangalore features numerous gardens and parks, earning it the nickname 'The Garden City'. Being an information technology center, the city has also earned another nickname: 'The Silicon Valley of India'.

The Mysore District has made a name for itself through its silk work. The creation of 'Mysore silk' greatly pushed the progress of the Indian silk industry and aided the country in overtaking China and Japan in the production of mulberry silk.

Landmarks

The **Gol Gumbaz** at Bijapur has the second largest dome in the world which is comparable to that of St. Peter's in Rome.

At a distance of 140 kms from Bangalore, Mysore has always enchanted tourists and visitors with its magnificent palaces, beautiful gardens and rich cultural heritage. The **Mysore Palace** is one of the largest palaces of its kind in India, and one of the most splendid. The palace has now been converted into a museum, which treasures the souvenirs, paintings, jewellery, royal costumes and other items. The Golden Royal Elephant Throne, the Durbar Hall, and the Kalyan Mandap (wedding hall) are the main attractions here.

KERALA

Kerala is typically rated one of the most beautiful places on Earth. Keralites take great pride in the beauty of their land and call the state 'God's Own Country'.

Kerala is said to be a fusion of 'kera' (coconut palm tree) and 'alam' (land or location). Another theory is that the name originated from the phrase 'chera alam' (Land of the Chera). Natives of Kerala, known as Keralites or Malayalis, thus refer to their land as Keralam.

With its principal language as **Malayalam**, the capital of Kerala is **Thiruvananthapuram**. Kerala has many achievements to its credit. Kerala has the highest literacy rate, highest female to male ratio, the highest quality of life index, and the lowest infant mortality rate of any state in India. This feat is an even greater marvel considering how densely populated the state is. Even its healthcare system has garnered international acclaim.

The State also takes a serious interest in the development of its culture. **Kathakali**-from katha (story) and 'kali' (performance is one of the major dance forms. Carnatic music dominates Keralite traditional music.

Kerala celebrates the festival known as the Great Elephant March. Beginning with a ceremony in Kochi, the festivities include elephant rides, an assembly of 101 elephants, elephant feeding ceremonies, and Chundan Vallom races also called the 'snake boat' races (a sort of water-chariot race) held every year during the festival Onam.

Landmarks

The Kerala backwaters are a chain of brackish lagoons and lakes lying parallel to the Arabian Sea coast (or Malabar Coast) of Kerala state in southern India. The backwaters have a unique ecosystem - freshwater from the rivers meets the seawater from the Arabian Sea. The backwaters are known as a major tourist destination.

The **Kovalam** beach is one of the best known in Kerala. The Periyar Game Sanctuary surrounds the Periyar Lake. A variety of wildlife may be seen either from lodges or viewing huts.

MADHYA PRADESH

Madhya Pradesh, the second largest Sate in India, often called the Heart of India, is a state in central India which geographically occupies a pivotal position in the country. Just as its name implies, Madhya Pradesh is in the middle (madhya) of India. Its capital is **Bhopal** and the principal language spoken is **Hindi**.

Landmarks

Ujjain, the oldest and holiest city of Parmar kings, also associated with Ashoka, Guptas and Vikramaditya has the Mahakaleshwar Temple. Every 12 years Ujjain has the greatest fair **Kumbh**, or Simhastha, as it is locally called. This is one of the four in the country, the others being at Haridwar, Allahabad and Nasik.

Sanchi, situated in the state of Madhya Pradesh, is a religious place with historical and archaeological significance. Sanchi is famous in the world for stupas, monolithic Asokan pillar, temples, monasteries and sculptural wealth dating from 3rd century BC to 12th century AD. The largest stupa, (large hemispherical domes, containing a central chamber, in which the relics of the Buddha were placed) known as the Great Stupa, is surrounded by a railing with four carved gateways facing all the four directions of the compass.

Chitrakoot Falls on the Indravati River in Bastar are a must see in Madhya Pradesh while a tour of this State could probably end at **Khajuraho**. Temples of Khajuraho are world famous for their architectural art and have been declared world heritage by UNESCO.

MAHARASHTRA

Located in West India, Maharashtra is the third largest state in the country. Its capital is the ever growing **Mumbai** (earlier Bombay) and its principal language is **Marathi**. The State has been identified as the country's powerhouse and Mumbai, its capital as the centre point of India's financial and commercial markets. **Pune**, the second largest city in Maharashtra, and the 7th largest in India, is the state's cultural and heritage capital. **Nagpur** - the 'orange city' as it is known - is located in the heart of India, and is the second administrative capital of Maharashtra. **Kolhapur** city situated in the south west corner of Maharashtra provides the location for the Mahalakshmi Temple. The city has strong cultural identity and lends its name to many common terms like Kolhapuri Chappal, Kolhapuri lavangi mirchi, Kolhapuri gur and Kolhapuri cuisine. Kolhapur is also known as 'Kalapur' for being home for artists (painters, singers, Marathi cinema etc).

The world famous Hindi Film industry Bollywood is in Maharashtra located in the economic capital of India Mumbai. The Marathi film industry was once placed in Kolhapur but now is spread out through Mumbai too.

Landmarks

About 107 km from the city of Aurangabad in Maharashtra, are the rock-cut caves of **Ajanta** nestled in a panoramic gorge, in the form of a gigantic horseshoe. A set of 29 caves, Ajanta is among the finest examples of some of the earliest Buddhist architecture, cave paintings and sculptures. Near this, there are 34 cave temples and monasteries at **Ellora**, excavated out of the vertical face of an escarpment. It is situated 26 km north of Aurangabad. Sculptors, inspired by Buddhism, Jainism and Hinduism, created elaborate rock carvings. Declared as World Heritage Sites by UNESCO since 1983, the paintings and sculptures of Ajanta and Ellora, considered masterpieces of Buddhist religious art, have had a great influence in the development of art in India.

The **Elephanta Caves** serve as a great tourist attraction in the vicinity of the large Mumbai metropolis. The Elephanta Island is located 10 km away from the Gateway of India at Mumbai in Maharashtra. This cave temple is dedicated to Lord Shiva.

The **Gateway of India** is one of Mumbai's best-known sites. Ceremonially built for the visit of King George V and Queen Mary in 1911, the arches also saw the departure of Britain from India. The last British troops left newly Independent India by sea and marched through the arches in their exit.

Some of the famous hill stations within the state are **Lonavala**, **Khandala**, **Mahabaleshwar** and **Panchgani**. These lend themselves to panoramic views of the valley.

TAMIL NADU

India's eleventh largest state, Tamil Nadu, is located in extreme southern India. Its capital is **Chennai**. **Tamil** is the official language of Tamil Nadu and is one of the two classical languages of India, the other being Sanskrit. Tamil is also one of the national languages of India.

Unique cultural features like **Bharatanatyam** (dance), **Tanjore painting**, and Tamil architecture were developed and continue to be practiced in Tamil Nadu. Bharatnatyam has been exported to the far reaches of the globe, with a strong base in Europe. Bharatanatyam is a classical dance and is thought to have been created by Bharata Muni, a Hindu sage, who wrote the Natya Shastra, the most important ancient treatise on classical Indian dance.

Tamil Nadu is also home to the Tamil film industry, the second largest film industry in India alongside Bollywood (Hindi films) and Tollywood (Telugu films). Chennai has often been referred to as Kollywood, a combination of Hollywood and Kodambakkam, the section of Chennai that houses cinema-related facilities.

Pongal, also called as Tamizhar Thirunaal (festival of Tamils), a four-day harvest festival, is the most celebrated festival of Tamil Nadu. Festivals of Tamil Nadu are celebrated with fervour unlike many other places. The Mahamagam festival comes once every twelve years, and the Arubathimoobar festival includes a procession of the 63 saints of Shiva.

Landmarks

Two hill stations, **Ootacamund** (Ooty) and **Kodaikanal** in the Nilgiri and Palni hills respectively are famous destination spots. **Kanyakumari**, the southern most tip of peninsular India, is famous for its distinct and beautiful sunrise. It also has a World Heritage site which comprises of the three great 11th and 12th century Chola Temples i.e. the **Brihadisvara temples** of Thanjavur, **Gangaikondacholisvaram**, and the **Airatesvara temple** at Darasuram. The three Chola temples in India are an exemplary production in the Dravidian style of temple architecture. In the heart of the ancient city of **Madurai** (more than 2,500 years old) lies the **Meenakshi-Sundareshwarar** temple which is dedicated to goddess Meenakshi, the consort of Lord Shiva. It has long been the focus of both Indian and international tourist attraction as well as one of the most important places of Hindu pilgrimage. For the people of Madurai, the temple is the very center of their cultural and

religious life. The folklore states that Meenakshi was the daughter of King Malayadwaja Pandya and Queen Kanchanamala, who was born after performing several yagnas (sacrificial rites). The three-year old girl emerged out of the fire during the final yagna. The princess Meenakshi grew to be a beautiful young woman of great valour who conquered several lands and challenged the mightiest kings. It was then revealed that the princess was actually an incarnation of Parvati who came to earth to honour a promise given to Kanchanamala in her previous life. Thus Shiva came to Madurai as Sundareshwarar to marry Meenakshi and the two ruled over the kingdom for many years before they left for their heavenly abode from the spot where the temple now stands.

MANIPUR

A relatively small state, Manipur sits as almost a literal pit of paradise. The name Manipur literally means 'a jeweled land'. Jawaharlal Nehru described the state as being the 'Jewel of India'.

Situated in the north eastern part of India, Manipur's capital is **Imphal** & the principal language is **Manipuri**. The Meiteis, who live primarily in the state's valley region, are one of the main ethnic groups. Their language, Meiteilon (also known as Manipuri), was recognised as one of India's national languages in 1992.

Manipuri passion for art, particularly the creation of clothes and garments, is astounding. Nearly every household possesses a loom. Manipuri dance is one of the major Indian classical dance forms.

Imphal has two war cemeteries, a museum displaying tribal artefacts, Kwairamb Bazaar (a woman's market where the ladies who sell are called Ima), the Rajah's Palace and Kangra Fort, besides many other places to see.

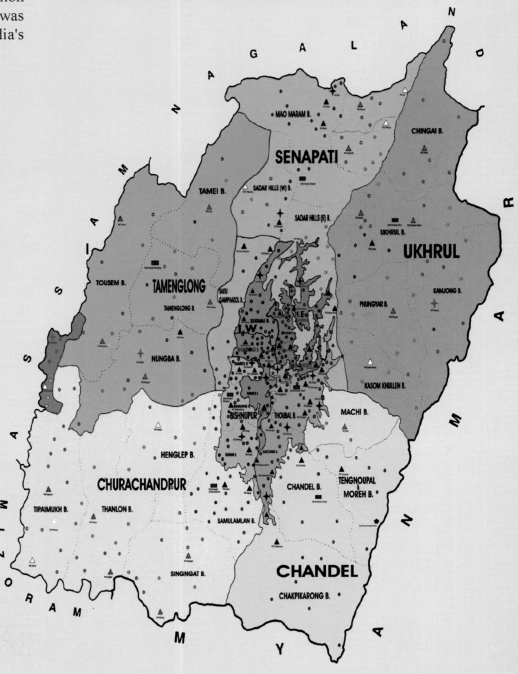

MIZORAM

Located on the far branch of northeast India, Mizoram's capital is **Aizwal** and the principal languages spoken in this state are **Mizo** and **English**. Mizoram's 90.27 % literacy rate is second highest among Indian states after Kerala.

Mizo enthusiasm for celebratory dancing cannot possibly be understated, considering the existence of the **Khuallam** (a dance for honoring visitors or guests) and the **Chheih Lam** (a dance for the glorious end of the workday).

30% of Mizoram is covered with wild bamboo forests, many of which are largely unexploited. Mizoram harvests 40% of India's 80 million-ton annual bamboo crop. The highest peak in Mizoram is the **Blue Mountain** (Phawngpui) with a height of 2210 meters.

NAGALAND

Situated in the eastern part of India, Nagaland's capital, **Kohima** is often described as the 'Highland City' and the **'Misty City'**. The official languages of the state are English and Nagamese.

The largest city of **Dimapur** is also known as the **'Gateway of Nagaland'**, 'The Commercial Hub (of Nagaland) and 'Melting Pot'. Nearly 90% of the Nagaland population leads an agrarian lifestyle, typically growing rice or corn. Music and dance are an intrinsic part of Naga life. Folk songs and ballads eulogising bravery, beauty, love, generosity, etc., are transmitted from generation to generation. Likewise, dancing is an integral part of every festive occasion. Feasting, singing, dancing and merrymaking invariably accompany festivals. Some of the important festivals are Sekrenyi, Moatsu, Tokhu Emong and Tuluni.

Weaving is a traditional art handed down through generations in Nagaland. Each of the major tribes has its own unique designs and colours, producing shawls, shoulder bags, decorative spears, table mats, wood carvings and bamboo works.

ARUNACHAL PRADESH

MON

LONGLENG

MOKOKCHUNG

TUENSANG

ASSAM

WOKHA

ZUNHEBOTO

KIPHIRE

MYANMAR

DIMAPUR

KOHIMA

PHEK

PEREN

MANIPUR

ORISSA

Orissa, the land of Oriyas, was known as Kalinga in ancient days. It is a state located on the east coast of India, by the Bay of Bengal. Orissa is the ninth largest state by area and the eleventh largest by population. **Oriya** is the official and most widely spoken language. Orissa's capital is **Bhubaneshwar**, also called the 'city of temples'. There were once over a thousand of them, a large number are still standing and are active today. The Lingraj Temple built to the glory of Shiva is one of the most impressive temples. Orissa is also home to the Hirakud Dam, one of the longest dams in the world. The famous classical dance form, Odissi originated in Orissa. Odissi or Orissi music is usually classified as a kind of Hindustani classical music of northern India, although some aspects of Odissi are quite distinct. Odissi has a long, unbroken tradition of 2,000 years, and finds mention in the Natyashastra of Bharatamuni, possibly written circa 200 BC.

Landmarks

Puri is a holy city and the site of the annual festival of the deity Jagannath. The Jagannath Temple which is often called, the 'White Pagoda' is one of the four Dhams (holy places) of Hinduism. The world-famous 'car festival' (rath yatra) occurs in Puri.

Konark Sun Temple, located in the eastern State of Orissa near the sacred city of Puri, is dedicated to the sun God or Surya. It is a monumental representation of the sun God Surya's chariot; its 24 wheels are decorated with symbolic designs and it is led by a team of six horses.

It is a masterpiece of Orissa's medieval architecture and one of India's most famous Brahman sanctuaries.

Chilka Lake, a brackish water coastal lake on the Bay of Bengal, south of the mouth of the Mahanadi River, is the largest coastal lake in India. It is protected by the Chilka Lake Bird Sanctuary, which harbors over 150 migratory and resident species of birds.

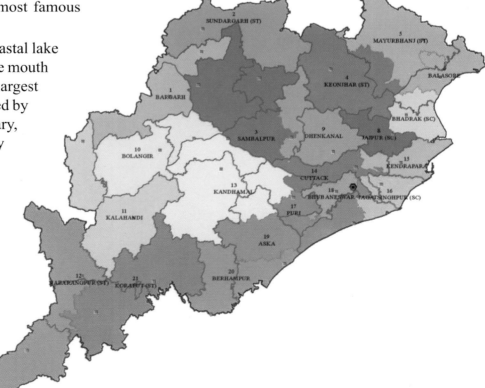

PUNJAB

The state which shares its capital, **Chandigarh**, with Haryana, is located in northwest India. The official language of Punjab is **Punjabi** and the state is considered to have the best infrastructure in India, this includes road, rail, air and river transport links that are extensive throughout the region. Punjab also has the lowest poverty rate in India and has won the best state performance award.

The word 'Punjab' is a combination of the Persian words 'panj' Five, and '?b' Water, giving the literal meaning of the Land of Five Rivers. The five rivers after which Punjab is named are the Beas, Jhelum, Chenab, Ravi and Sutlej.

One of Punjab's most treasured traditions is the art known as phullkari (flowering). The craft involves creating flowery designs and surfaces using the very basic tools of a needle and silk thread. The official dance of the state is **Bhangra**.

Landmarks

Sri Harmandir Sahib, also known as Sri Darbar Sahib or **Golden Temple**, (on account of its scenic beauty and golden coating), situated in Amritsar, is the most sacred temple for Sikhs. Guru Arjan Sahib, the Fifth Guru, conceived the idea of creating a central place of worship for the Sikhs and he himself designed the architecture of Sri Harmandir Sahib. The temple is square and has a door each on the East, West, North and South. In this way it is accessible to every person without any distinction based on caste, creed, sex and religion. The Sheesh Mahal or the 'Palace of Mirrors' in Patiala was built by Maharaja Narinder Singh behind the main Moti Bagh Palace. The Palace was built in a forest with terraces, gardens, fountains and an artificial lake.

The Jallianwala Bagh is where on 13th April 1919, General Dyer fired on an unarmed crowd and killed over 300 people. The garden has a monument commemorating the event and has become a place of pilgrimage.

RAJASTHAN

Rajasthan, the largest State in India in terms of area, prior to independence, was known as Rajputana or the home of Rajputs-a martial community who ruled over this area for centuries. Its principal languages are **Hindi** and **Rajasthani**. The 'Pink City' of **Jaipur** (the city of jai or victory) is its capital.

Rajasthan is famous for the majestic forts, intricately carved temples and decorated *havelis*, which were built by kings in previous ages. The **Ghoomar** dance from Udaipur and **Kalbeliya** dance of Jaisalmer have gained international recognition. Folk music is a vital part of Rajasthani culture of which **Kathputali** is famous. Folk songs (commonly ballads which relate heroic deeds and love stories) and religious or devotional songs known as *bhajans* and *banis* (often accompanied by musical instruments like *dholak*, *sitar*, *sarangi* etc. are also very common.

Rajasthan is often considered a sentinel for India thanks to the **Thar Desert**. Stretching from Rajasthan into Pakistan, the Thar Desert, also known as the Great Indian Desert, contains wide spread sand dunes and is one of the harshest terrains in the world.

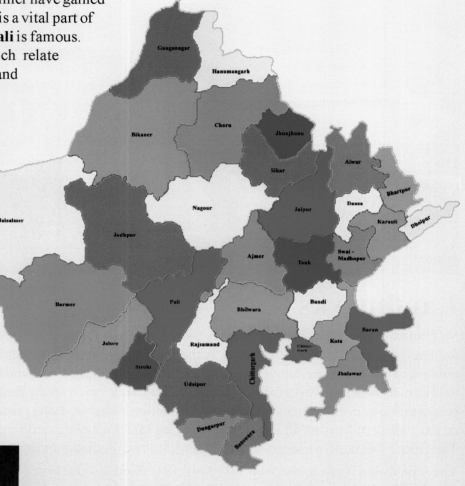

Landmarks

One of the world's oldest mountain ranges, the **Aravalli Range**, cradles the only hill station of Rajasthan, Mount Abu. Thanks to its lush plant life and beautiful surroundings, **Mount Abu** is also known as the 'Paradise of Rajasthan'. Wondrously carved in marble, the **Dilwara Jain temples** in Mount Abu enshrine various Jain 'Tirthankaras'. Constructed out of white marble, the temples are an outstanding example of Jain temple architecture.

Jaisalmer Fort was built in 1156 and is the second oldest in the state of Rajasthan. The fort, built by Rawal Jaisal, which crowns Trikuta hill, has its outer wall of palaces, houses and temples of soft yellow sandstone. Almost one quarter of the town's population resides inside the fort.

The 'Pink City' of Jaipur is noted for the ancient houses made of a type of sand stone dominated by a pink hue. Jaipur was not always pink. The original city was grey, edged with white borders and motifs. In honour of the visit of Prince Albert, it was ordered to be painted the traditional colour of welcome and has since remained the same.

One of the best sites, **Hawa Mahal** or Palace of Winds, famous for its beehive like structure, is an interplay of red and pink sand stone, carefully and painstakingly outlined with white borders and motifs. The palace is in fact not a real palace but an extraordinary façade of 953 airy windows earlier used by the ladies of the palace to watch the outside world - without being seen.

Sheesh Mahal or the Palace of Mirrors has walls, which are inlaid with exquisite mirrored motifs that dance to the flame of even a single candle. Another place called **Pushkar**, 150 kilometres from Jaipur is considered up in the hierarchy of Hindu places of pilgrimage. It is the site of the temple to Brahma, the Creator, of which there are very few. Every year a Pushkar festival is held which hundreds and thousands of pilgrims attend.

Jantar Mantar, **Chittorgarh Fort**, **Lake Palace Hotel**, **City Palaces**, **Jaisalmer Havelis** are part of the true architectural heritage of India. Other places within the state to visit are **Udaipur**, **Jodhpur**, **Jaisalmer**, **Bikaner**, **Ajmer** and **Alwar**.

SIKKIM

Located in the Eastern Himalayas, Sikkim is a landlocked Indian state. It is the least populous state in India and the second-smallest in area after Goa. With its capital as **Gangtok** meaning 'the hill made flat', its principal languages are **Lepcha**, **Bhutia**, **Limbu** and **Nepali**.

The name Sikkim is derived from Sukhim, which means 'happy home, a place of peace'. It is an ancient land also known as 'Indrakil' or 'garden of Indra', the king-God of heaven, in Hindu religious texts. Sikkim is also known as the hidden valley of rice.

Noodle-based dishes such as the thukpa, chowmein, thanthuk, fakthu, gyathuk and wonton are common in Sikkim. Momos, steamed dumplings filled with vegetable, buff (buffalo's meat) or pork and served with a soup are a popular snack.

Landmarks

The summit of the **Kanchenjunga** is the highest point and 3rd in the world. Locals of the state worship the Goddess of Mount Kanchenjunga as the protector of the state. Tashiding Monastery in West Sikkim is considered the holiest of all the monasteries in Sikkim. There is also an Orchid Sanctuary where over 250 different types of Orchids bloom in summer.

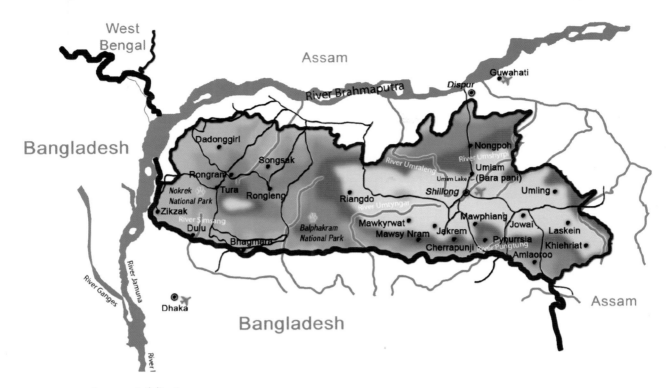

MEGHALAYA

The name Meghalaya literally means 'Abode of the Clouds'. An aptly given name, considering the rainfall and cloud cover of the region. **Shillong**, the capital of Meghalaya has been called the 'Scotland of the East', because of its climate and its location at an altitude of 4,900 feet. The principal languages spoken in the State are **Khasi**, **Garo** and **English**.

Tribal people make up the majority of Meghalaya's population. The Khasis are the largest group, followed by the Garos. Rich with vegetation, approximately 30% of the state is covered in forest land, and it is home to over 325 different species of orchids.

Meghalaya is the **wettest state** of India. The town of **Cherrapunji** in the Khasi Hills, south of capital Shillong, holds the world record for most rain in a calendar month, while the village of Mawsynram, near the town of Cherrapunji, holds the distinction of seeing the heaviest yearly rains.

The popular waterfalls in the state are the Elephant Falls, Shadthum Falls, Weinia falls, Bishop Falls, Nohkalikai Falls, Langshiang Falls and Sweet Falls. The hot springs at Jakrem near Mawsynram are believed to have curative and medicinal properties.

TRIPURA

Situated in North East India, Tripura is the third smallest state of the country. Its capital is **Agartala** and the principal languages spoken are **Bengali** and **Kokborak**. According to a historian, the word Tripura is a derivative from two different Kokborak words: 'twi' and 'pra'. Twi means water, pra means near. It is likely that the state bears the name Tripura from this fact that in ancient time the boundaries of Tripura extended up to the Bay of Bengal when its ruler held sway from the Garo Hills to the Arakan.

Tripura was never under British control during the occupation of India. Instead, it was a princely state under the control of its maharaja. This form of governance continued until India won its independence.

About 50% of the Tripura population lives in a tribal community. The tribal lifestyle extends right down to the essentials of art. One of the most basic instruments in traditional Tripura music is the bamboo flute.

Agartala has Ujjayana Place, Jagannath Temple, Laxmi Narayan Temple, and Uma Maheswari Temple amongst others.

UTTARAKHAND

Previously known as Uttaranchal, Uttarakhand became the 27th state of the Republic of India on 9th November, 2000. In January 2007, the name of the state was officially changed from Uttaranchal, its interim name, to Uttarakhand, according to the wishes of a large section of its people.

Literally North Country or Section in Sanskrit, Uttarakhand is also well known as the birthplace of the Chipko environmental movement. Its capital is **Dehradun** known for Forest Research Institute and Indian Military Academy. Its principal languages are **Hindi**, **Garhwali**, and **Kumaoni**.

The world-famous Kumbh Mela/Ardh Kumbh Mela is held in **Hardwar** at an interval of every twelfth/sixth year.

Landmarks

Corbett National Park is a must visit when one comes to the state. Rainforests and alpine forests cover a great portion of the state's Himalayan region and this region is home to many exotic and endangered species. Thanks to plant life, animal life, and an enjoyable climate, these forest regions are at the heart of Uttarakhand tourism.

To Uttarakhand, long called 'abode of the gods' (Devbhumi), belong some of the holiest Hindu shrines, and for more than a thousand years, pilgrims have been visiting the region in the hopes of salvation and purification from sin. **Gangotri** and **Yamunotri**, the sources of both the Ganges and Yamuna fall in the upper reaches of the state and together with **Badrinath** (dedicated to Vishnu) and **Kedarnath** (dedicated to Shiva) form the Chardham of Uttarakhand, one of Hinduism most spiritually auspicious pilgrimage circuits. **Rishikesh** near Haridwar is known as the pre-eminent yoga centre of India while the spectacular view from Hemkund is of special significance to Sikhs.

The world-famous Valley of Flowers, Pindari Glacier, Roop Kund, Dayara Bugyal, Auli, and hill stations like **Mussoorie**, **Dehradun**, **Chakrata**, **Nainital**, **Ranikhet**, **Bageshwar**, **Bhimtal**, **Kausani** are the important places of tourist interest.

UTTAR PRADESH

The fourth largest state in physical size, Uttar Pradesh sits in northern India. Its capital is **Lucknow** and the principal languages spoken are **Hindi** and **Urdu**. To get an idea of its massive size, the state of Uttar Pradesh is ten times as large as the nation of Belgium.

India's basic and distinct musical tradition was born in Uttar Pradesh. The two most popular instruments of Indian music - the *sitar* and the *tabla*, where both created in the state. It is also known for its dances and folk theatre forms which include *Raslila, Swang, Ramlila* (which includes enacting the entire Ramayana), *Nautanki, Naqal* (mimicry), *Khayal* and *Qawwali. Kathak*, a classical dance form, involving gracefully coordinated movements of feet along with entire body, grew and flourished in Uttar Pradesh.

Uttar Pradesh is famous for its rich heritage of art and craft. **Agra** and **Kanpur** are internationally known for their leather craft. **Firozabad**, the city of bangles, is also a hub for many glass accessories. **Kannauj** is well known for oriental perfumes, scents and rose water and for tobacco. **Khurja** is famous for its ceramics pottery. Lucknow, the capital, boasts of its cloth work and embroidery (chikkan) work on silk and cotton. **Mirzapur** and **Bhadohi** are known for carpets. **Moradabad** is well known for its metal ware, especially brass artifacts. **Saharanpur** is known all over India and abroad for wood carving items produced here. Varanasi is famous for its banarasi saris and silk.

Landmarks

The city of Agra, which gives access to three world heritage sites: **Taj Mahal**, **Agra Fort** and **Fatehpur Sikri**. The Taj Mahal is sheer poetry in marble. Majesty and magnificence, unrivalled, the Taj Mahal is the only one of its kind across the world. This is the monumental labour of love of a great ruler for his beloved queen - the ultimate realization of Emperor Shahjahan's dream. It is considered one of the wonders of the world.

Near the gardens of Taj Mahal stands the important Mughal monument known as the Red Fort of Agra. This powerful fortress of red sandstone encompasses within its enclosure walls, the imperial city of the Mughal rulers. There are a number of exquisite buildings like **Moti Masjid, Diwan-E-Am, Diwan-E-Khaas, Musamman Burj** - where Mughal Emperor Shah Jahan died, Jahangir's Palace, Khaas Mahal and Sheesh Mahal. Agra Fort, an excellent example of Mughal architecture, is one of the few UNESCO World Heritage Sites in India.

The royal city at Fatehpur Sikri, situated 26 miles west of Agra, Uttar Pradesh, was built under the orders of the great Mughal Emperor Akbar. In honour of Saint Shaikh Salim Chisti, Akbar founded a magnificent city on Sikri ridge.

The holy cities of **Varanasi**, **Ayodhya**, **Mathura**, and **Allahabad**, are located on the banks of sacred rivers Ganga and the Yamuna. Millions of tourists and pilgrims visit these holy cities. Magh Mela is held at Allahabad in January when the people come in large number to have a dip in the holy Sangam. Also, the biggest congregation, perhaps of the world, Kumbha Mela is held at Allahabad every twelfth year, where over 10 million Hindu pilgrims congregate - the largest gathering of human beings in the world. Ardh kumbh Mela is held every sixth year.

Varanasi is widely considered to be the second oldest city in the world after Jerusalem. It is famous for its ghats (bathing steps along the river), that remain bustling year round with devotees from all over India and beyond, who want to take a holy dip in the sacred Ganges River. Ayodhaya is the birthplace of Lord Rama and is considered to be an important pilgrimage centre.

About 13 km from Varanasi is the historically important town of **Sarnath**. Gautama Buddha gave his first sermon at Sarnath after his enlightenment and hence it is an important pilgrimage site for the Buddhists. Sarnath is home to the Ashoka Pillar and the Lion Capital, both important archaeological artifacts with national significance. Lucknow which is named after Lakshman, younger brother of Lord Rama, the hero of the famous epic "Ramayana", city stands on river Gomati. The city is home to 'Bara Imambara', a historical edifice with such a marvelous architecture that even modern architects seem to be perplexed by its design. The Bara Imambara is an interesting building. It is neither a mosque, nor a mausoleum, but a huge building having interesting elements within it. The building has an amazing maze of corridors hidden in between its walls. This dense, dark maze called the 'bhul bhulaiya' is a network of more than 1000 labyrinthine passages, some of which have dead-ends, some end at precipitous drops while others lead to entrance or exit points. Help of an "approved" guide is recommended if one wants a tour of the secret labyrinth without getting lost.

WEST BENGAL

The region that is now West Bengal was a part of a number of empires and kingdoms during the past two millennia. The British East India Company cemented their hold on the region following the Battle of Plassey, and the city of Kolkata, then Calcutta, served for many years as the capital of British India. Today, West Bengal in India has its capital called **Kolkata** and the principal language spoken here is **Bengali**.

West Bengal also has a heritage in North Indian classical music. 'Rabindrasangeet', songs composed and set into tune by Rabindranath Tagore and 'Nazrulgeeti' (by Kazi Nazrul Islam) are popular. Durga Puja is the most important festival along with Kali Puja in the state.

Mainstream Hindi films are popular, as are films from the Bengali cinema industry, dubbed 'Tollywood'. Tollygunj in Kolkata is the location of Bengali movie studios and the name 'Tollywood' is derived from that name. The Bengali film industry is also known for art films or Indy films. Its long tradition of filmmaking has produced acclaimed directors like Satyajit Ray, Mrinal Sen, Tapan Sinha and Ritwik Ghatak. Contemporary directors include Buddhadev Dasgupta, Goutam Ghose, Aparna Sen and Rituparno Ghosh.

Kolkata is the only city in India to have trams as a mode of transport and these are operated by the Calcutta Tramways Company. Bengalis make distinctive sweetmeats from milk products, including Rôshogolla, Chômchôm, Kalojam and several kinds of Pithe.

Landmarks

Kolkata was built around Fort William. On the western side of the fort is the Strand and the Hoogly River and on the eastern side is the Maidan. The Maidan is a huge open park surrounding Fort William. Earlier no building was permitted to be made on this Maidan, but today the main building on this Maidan is the Victoria Memorial. **Victoria Memorial** is one of the famous and beautiful monuments of Kolkata built between 1906 and 1921 to commemorate Queen Victoria's 25-year reign in India. This huge white-marble museum, made from Makrana marbles from Rajasthan, is filled with a vast collection of remnants from the period of British Empire rule in India. The Botanical Gardens in Howrah, Kolkata has one of the largest Banyan trees in the world.

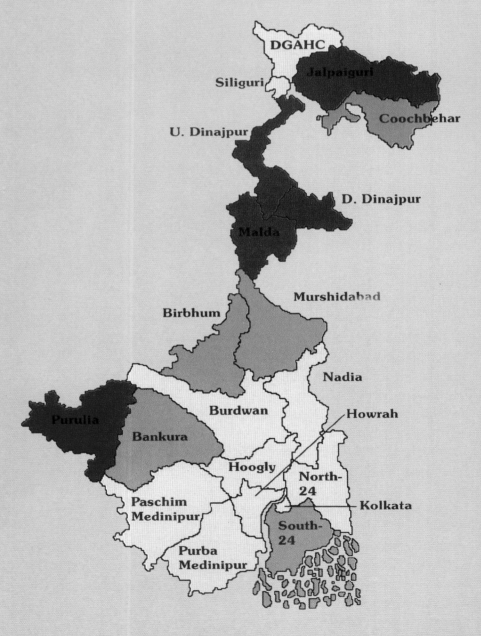

South of Calcutta begin the Sunderbans, 'beautiful forest', in Bengali, formed by the delta of the Ganga and the Brahmaputra. Two thirds of this area is in Bangladesh. The Sunderbans are a marshy mangrove jungle, the largest estuarine forest in the world.

Darjeeling is one of the biggest hill stations in West Bengal. Darjeeling 'orthodox' tea is very famous and among the most expensive. An Observatory Hill is perhaps the oldest built-up site in Darjeeling.

Kalimpong, east of Darjeeling has two Buddhist monasteries: Tharpa Choling at Tirpai (largest) and the Zang-dog Palrifo Brang Monastery on Durpin Dara Hill. Kalimpong is well known for its street markets.

The **Tarakeshwar Temple** built around a black stone lingam of Tarakeshwar Babu, an avatar of Shiva, 57 km west of Calcutta is one of West Bengal's most active pilgrimage centres.

North of Vishnupur (further west from Calcutta) is Shantiniketan. Rabindranath Tagore's father had founded an ashram here. It became one of the hubs of intellectual life of India.

UNION TERRITORIES

ANDAMAN & NICOBAR ISLANDS

Located in the Indian Ocean, in the southern reaches of the Bay of Bengal, it comprises two island groups - the Andaman Islands and the Nicobar Islands - which separate the Andaman Sea to the east from the Indian Ocean. The principal languages of the state are Hindi, Nicobarese, Bengali, Tamil, Malayalam and Telugu.

The name Andaman presumably comes from Hanuman, who is a powerful Hindu God. The name Nicobar is Malayalam for 'land of the people'. The capital is called **Port Blair**. It was named after Lt. Reginald Blair who conducted a survey of the area in 1789.

Landmarks

The **Cellular Jail**, now a museum where 400 freedom fighters were held during the struggle for independence, is a massive white washed building which faces the ocean.

The Zoo on Haddo Promontory has salt water crocodiles, hornbills and crab eating monkeys. Other places of interest are the Anthropological Museum and a Burmese temple at Phoenix Bay. There is also Vyper Island where executions used to take place.

The other important places of tourist interest are Marine Museum, Water Sports Complex, Gandhi Park, North Bay, Ross Island, Chidiyatapu, (Bird watching), Red Skin Island, Corbyn's Cove Beach, Islands like Neil Island, Havelock Island, Cinque, Little Andaman, Diglipur (Ross & Smith), etc.

CHANDIGARH

Often called City Beautiful, Chandigarh is a city in India that serves as the capital of two states, Punjab and Haryana, and is a union territory of India. The city nestles in a picturesque setting in the foothills of Shivalik hills. Its capital is **Chandigarh** and the principal languages spoken are Hindi, Punjabi and English.

Chandigarh City itself is notable for its infrastructure and design. It was designed by the famous architect, Le Corbusier assisted by his cousin, Jeanneret. Corbusier designed most of its important public buildings including the Secretariat, the Legislative Assembly and the High Court.

The city derives its name from Chandi Mandir, a temple of goddess Chandi, located in nearby Panchkula District of Haryana. The word Chandigarh literally means 'the fort of Chandi'.

Important tourist places are Rock Garden, Rose Garden, Sukhna Lake, Museum and Art Gallery, City Museum, Tower of Shadows, Geometric Hill Museum of Evolution, Kala Gram, Log Huts, Nepli Forests, Fitness Trails (in Leisure Valley), National Gallery of Portraits, Central Plaza, International Doll Museum and Smriti Upvan.

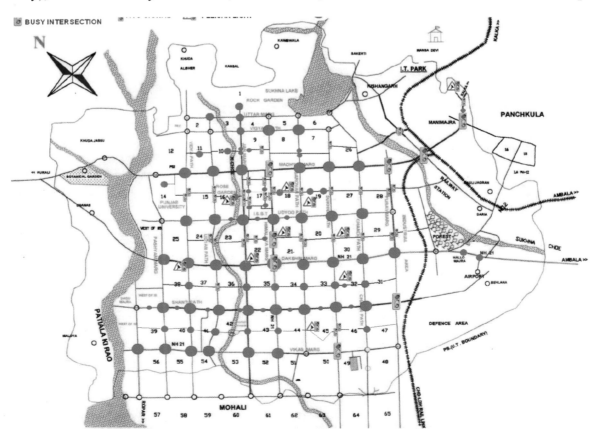

DADRA AND NAGAR HAVELI

The two regions - Dadra and Nagar Haveli are separated from each other by a few kilometers. Both lie on the West coast, at the mouth of the Daman Ganga River. The principal languages of Dadra and Nagar Haveli are **Gujarati** and **Hindi**. Their capital is called Silvassa.

The prominent places of tourist interest are Tadekeshwar Shiva Mandir, Bindrabin, Deer Park at Khanvel, Vanganga Lake and Island Garden, Dadra, Vanvihar Udhyan Mini Zoo, Bal Udhyan, Tribal Museum, and Hirvavan Garden at Silvassa. To encourage tourism activities, some traditional and modern cultural activities like celebration of Tarpa Festival, Kite festival, World Tourism day, etc., are organized every year.

Tourist Spots to be seen in and around Silvassa town are Tribal Museum, Temples - Ram Temple, Balaji Temple, Ayyappa Temple, Church, Van Dhara Garden, Hirva Van Garden (both these gardens are near the river). Madhuban Dam is situated on the river Daman Ganga. Going southwards, approximately 18 KM from Silvassa a small village called Bindrabin (in local dialect), some call it Vrundavan is Temple of Lord Shiva.

DAMAN AND DIU

Daman and Diu is a union territory in India. For over 450 years, these coastal enclaves on the Arabian Sea coast were part of Portuguese India, along with Goa, Dadra and Nagar Haveli. The principal language spoken here is Gujarati and the capital is **Daman**.

In Daman places that one can visit are Bom Jesus Chruch, Our Lady of Sea Church; Our Lady of Remedios Church; Forts of Moti Daman and Nani Daman; Jampore and Devka Beaches; Public Garden and Moti Daman Jetty, Pargola Garden, Moti Daman, Amusement Park, Devka; Damanganga Tourist Complex, Kachigam; Satya Sagar Udyan, Mirasol Garden, Mirasal Water Park.

In Diu, St. Paul's Church; Diu Fort and Panikota Fort; Nagoa and Chakratirth and Children's park at Ghoghla and Summer House are famous places of tourist interest.

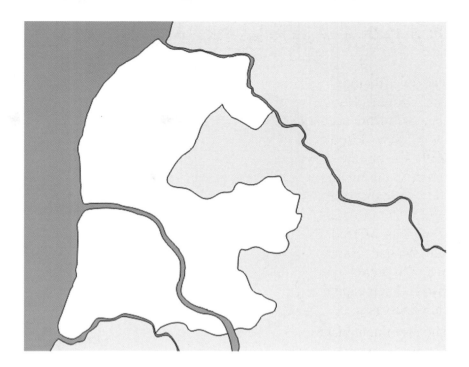

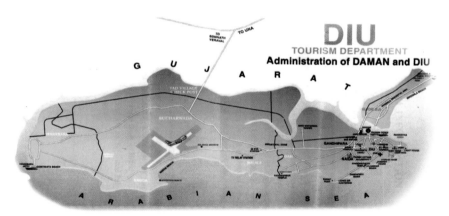

Landmarks

The **Church of Bom Jesus** was started in 1559 but consecrated in 1603. It was a parish church in the early days of the Portuguese rule. The monument is a living tribute to the craftsmanship of Portuguese artisans in ornate and intricate design. The main feature of the church is its richly carved main south door with the elevated facade, lofty ceiling, embellished with the statues of six saints.

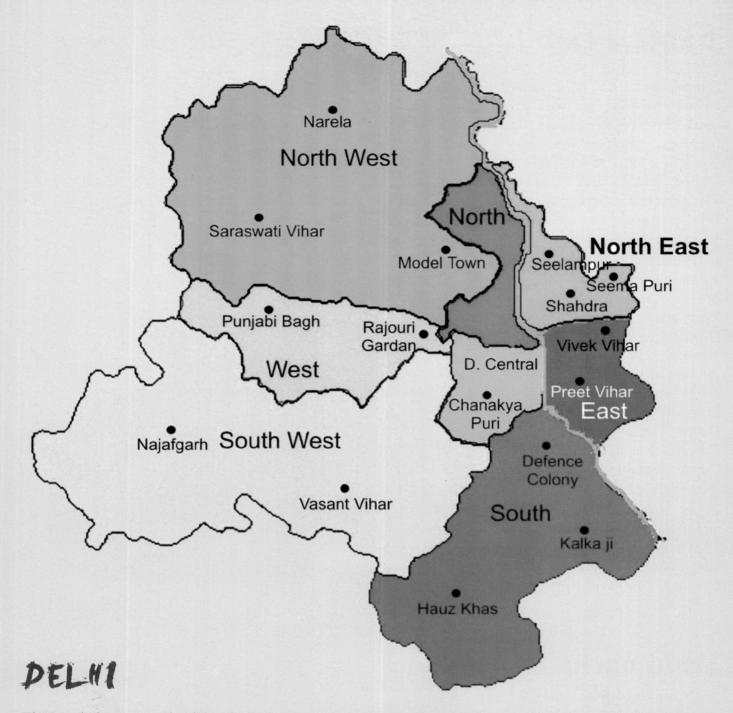

DELHI

The Mughal emperor Shahjahan built the city, now known as 'Old Delhi', to serve as the capital of the Mughal Empire from 1649 to 1857. After the British Raj took control of India during the 19th century, Calcutta became the capital until George V announced in 1911 that it was to move back to Delhi. A new capital city, New Delhi, was built during the 1920s. When India gained independence from British rule in 1947, New Delhi was declared its capital and seat of government.

It's commonly viewed that Delhi is an eponym of Dhillu, a king who ruled the area in ancient times. Some historians believe that the name is derived from Dilli, a version of dehleez or dehali-Hindi for 'threshold'- and symbolic of the city as a Gateway to the Indo-Gangetic Plain. A third belief is that Delhi is derived from Dhillika, the name of the first medieval township of Delhi, located on the southwestern border of the present Union Territory of Delhi, in Mehrauli.

Delhi is the second largest metropolis in India, with a population of 17 million, and a federally-administered union territory officially known as the National Capital Territory of Delhi (NCT). The principal languages spoken in Delhi are **Hindi**, **Punjabi**, **Urdu** and **English**. The city was also host to the 2010 Commonwealth Games, the largest multi-sport event ever held in the city.

Landmarks

Three World Heritage Sites-the **Red Fort**, **Qutub Minar** and **Humayun's Tomb**-are located in Delhi. Other monuments include the **India Gate**, the **Jantar Mantar** (an 18th century astronomical observatory) and the **Purana Qila** (a 16th century fortress).

Delhi's famous Red Fort is known by that name because of the red stone with which it is built and it is one of the most magnificent palaces in the world. India's history is also closely linked with this fort. It was from here that the British deposed the last Mughal ruler, Bhadur Shah Zafar, marking the end of the three century long Mughal rule. It was also from its ramparts that the first Prime Minister of India, Pandit Jawharlal Nehru, announced to the nation that India was free from colonial rule.

Qutub Minar in red and buff sandstone is the highest tower in India. Built in the 13th century, the magnificent tower stands in the capital, Delhi. With a height of 72.5m, it is an architectural marvel of ancient India. UNESCO has declared the highest stone tower in India as a World Heritage Site.

A fine specimen of the great Mughal architecture in the capital Delhi is the Humayun's tomb. Built in 1570, the tomb is of particular cultural significance as it was the first garden-tomb on the Indian subcontinent. The structure is built with red sandstone, but white and black marble has been used in the borders. This historic monument was erected by Humayun's queen Hamida Banu Begam (Haji Begam) and it is believed that she designed the tomb.

India Gate, an important monument of the city, is a memorial built in commemoration of more than 80,000 Indian soldiers who were killed during World War I. The monument is an imposing 42 meters high arch and was designed by the famous architect Edwin Lutyens. India gate was earlier named All India War Memorial. The building is made of red stone that rises in stages. On top of the arch, INDIA is written on both sides. At the base of the India gate there is another memorial, the Amar Jawan Jyoti that was added after independence. This eternal flame was lighted in commemoration of the unknown soldiers who laid their lives to serve this nation. Every year on 26th January India Gate stands witness to the Republic Day parade.

Delhi's Jantar Mantar is the first of the five observatories built with large masonry instruments by Sawai Jai Singh II of Jaipur. He was a keen astronomer and a noble in the Mughal court. Dissatisfied by the errors of brass and metal astronomical instruments, under patronage from the emperor, he set on himself the task of correcting the existing astronomical tables and updating the almanac with more reliable instruments,

Purana Quila (Old Fort) in Delhi has been built on a small hill standing on the banks of river Yamuna with its massive rubble wall and imposing gateway houses. The structure houses a mosque, which has a double storied octagonal tower. According to Hindu literature the fort marks the site of Indraprastha, the magnificent capital of the Pandavas.

Apart from these World Heritage Sites, other important part of Delhi's are the Rashtrapati Bhavan, the official residence of the President of India, located at the west end of the Rajpath in New Delhi with the India gate

at the opposite end. Designed by Edwin Landseer Lutyens, this palatial building was the erstwhile residence of the British Viceroy. Few official residential premises of the State Heads in the world will match the Rashtrapati Bhavan in terms of its size, vastness and its magnificence.

The **Laxminarayan Temple**, **Akshardham** and the **Bahá'í Lotus Temple** are examples of modern architecture. A lotus-shaped structure in Delhi called the Bahá'í Mashriqu'l-Adhkar is better known as the "Lotus Temple". The lotus flower represents the manifestation of God. The Lotus Temple proves to be a remarkable fusion of ancient concept, modern engineering skill, and architectural inspiration. The Temple, with

its total absence of idols, leaves people bewildered, yet satisfied. Visitors express perplexity at the absence of any deity and yet are awed by the beauty and grandeur of the edifice.

Jama Masjid (the mosque of Friday), which stands across the road from Red Fort is the country's largest and perhaps it's most magnificent mosque. The great mosque of Old Delhi is the final architectural extravagance of the Mughal Emperor Shah Jahan with a courtyard capable of holding 25,000 devotees. Its also known as 'Masjid-i-Jahanuma' or 'Mosque commanding view of the world'. Jama Masjid is the replica of Moti Masjid in Agra. It combines the best of Hindu and Muslim styles of architecture.

LAKSHADWEEP

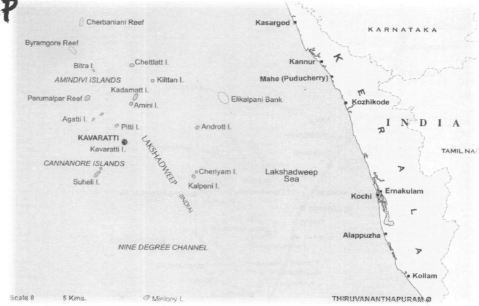

The name of the archipelago literally translates as "hundred thousand islands" (laksha is "one hundred thousand", dweep is "island"). With its Capital as Kavaratti, the principal languages spoken are Jeseri (Dweep Bhasha) and Mahal.

Lakshwadeep is the smallest union territory of India located 200 to 300 km off of the coast of Kerala in the Arabian Sea. It is an archipelago of 27 coral islands and of open reefs. Of the Islands, only 10 are inhabited by people. The language often spoken here is **Malayalam**. Coconut is the only major crop with a production of 553 lakh nuts per year. Coconut farming and fishing serve as the main occupations.

Tourism in Lakshadweep is developing into an important industry. Important tourist places are Agatti, Kalpeni, Kadmat, Kavaratti and Minicoy, etc. Bangaram, one of the uninhabited islands, provides facilities for water sports in the fair season.

PUDUCHERRY

This formerly, French-ruled town consisting of four non-contiguous enclaves, or districts, and named for the largest, Pondicherry (known in Tamil as Puducherry) is now one of India's Union Territories. The territory of Puducherry comprises of the former French establishment Puducherry, Karaikal, Mahe and Yanam, which lie scattered in South India. Puducherry means "New village" in the Tamil language. It is also known as The French Riviera of the East (La Côte d'Azur de l'Est).

Located about 160 Km South of Chennai, Puducherry, the former French Colony of the early 18th century, is a charming Indian town with a few enduring pockets of French Culture, and an *Ashram* set beside the sea. Together with the other former French enclaves of Karaikal (also in Tamil Nadu), Mahe (Kerala), Yanam (Andhra Pradesh), it now forms the Union, Territory of Pondicherry. The uniqueness of this town invariably lies in skillful town planning and Franco Tamil architecture. The town is built on the model of 'bastide', a fortified French coastal town of the late 18th century.

Other places that can be seen in Puducherry are Auroville, Aurobindo Ashram, Chunnambar Boat House, Botanical Garden and the Puducherry museums.

INDIA AFTER INDEPENDENCE

INDIA AFTER INDEPENDENCE

Our country India became Independent on 15th August, 1947. It has been over 60 years now, since we gained Independence. Nearly two centuries of British rule ended at midnight on August 14, 1947 and a new era began in the history of India. On the morning of August 15, 1947, Prime Minister Jawaharlal Nehru hoisted the tricolour Indian flag at the top of the Red Fort (Lal Quila) in Delhi, amidst joyful celebrations by the people. Since then, this day is celebrated as Independence Day.

Mahatma Gandhi's death on 30th January, 1948 shocked the nation. After this event, there were many communal riots and soon, there was a problem of merging almost 600 princely states with the rest of the country. By 1961, the territorial and political integration of India was completed, even though it had taken over 14 years to do so.

INDIA BECOMES A REPUBLIC

When India became independent, the leaders of our country decided to prepare a written document called the Constitution. This Constitution provides guidelines to help the Government of India to run the country.

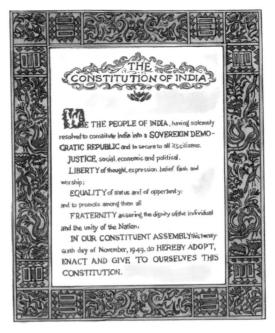

DID YOU KNOW?
The Indian Constitution, the longest in the world, consist of 397 articles and 12 schedules, which provides for a single citizenship for the whole of India.

THE CONSTITUTION PROVIDES

A set of rules to which the ordinary laws of the country must conform.

Lists the fundamental rights of every Indian, such as - freedom of thought, expression, belief, faith and worship. Justice to All, whether rich or poor, man or woman, irrespective of their social and economic status. The right to vote to all citizens above 18 years. The Constitution declares India to be a secular state. It does not have a state religion and honours all religions equally. The Supreme Court, consisting of the Chief Justice of India and other judges, is the guardian of the Constitution. Sometimes the rights mentioned in the Constitution can be restricted when there is an emergency of any kind or to preserve public order or national security, like in the case of the Emergency in June 1975. In order to make the Constitution of India unite people from different backgrounds and religions, after 3 years of debates and discussions, in November 1949, Dr. B. R. Ambedkar presented the first draft Constitution. The new Constitution came into force on 26th January, 1950 and India became a Sovereign Democratic Republic. Since then, **26th January** is celebrated as the **Republic Day**.

Dr. Rajendra Prasad became the first president and **Jawaharlal Nehru** the first Prime Minister of the Republic of India.

INDIA'S NATIONALSYMBOLS

Independent India also chose its national symbols like the **State Emblem** which is a replica of the Ashok pillar at Sarnath in which 4 lions are sitting with their backs to one another. The tricolour flag of the Congress made of three colours - Saffron, White and Green was adopted as the **National Flag**. The white in the middle has a chakra having 24 spokes in deep blue colour. Saffron symbolizes courage, sacrifice and renunciation. White stands for truth and purity - truth in our speech and purity of thought while the freshness of green represents life, faith and chivalry. The 24 spokes of the wheel are multiples of 8, representing the noble precepts of the Eight-Fold path taught by the Buddha. The wheel itself denotes unceasing motion and progress.

The **National Flower** of India is the **Lotus**, a symbol of beauty, purity and integrity. The status of the **National Animal** is enjoyed by the **Tiger** while the **National Bird** is the **Peacock**. **Jana-Gana-Mana**, the song written by Rabindranath Tagore, is the **National Anthem** and Vande Mataram composed by Bankim Chandra Chaterji is the **National Song**.

To summarize:

National Emblem - replica of the Ashok pillar at Sarnath

National Flag - tricolour made of Saffron, White and Green with a chakra in the middle on the white.

National Flower - Lotus

National Bird - Peacock

National Animal - Tiger

National Anthem - Jana-Gana-Mana, the song written by Rabindranath Tagore

National Song - Vande Mataram composed by Bankim Chandra Chaterji

सत्यमेव जयते

DEMOCRACY IN INDIA

Democracy in India took a giant step forward with the first general election in India from October 1951 to February 1952. India's election system was developed according to the Constitution which had created an Election Commission and a Chief Election Commissioner to conduct the elections.

People's response to the election was tremendous. What was remarkable was the wide participation of women. The Congress under the leadership of Jawaharlal Nehru swept the polls and Jawaharlal Nehru became the Prime Minister.

INDIA, THE LARGEST DEMOCRACY

India is now a Parliamentary democracy. It means that the people of India elect their leaders themselves who meet in what is called the Parliament and make laws for the country. No other democracy in the world has so many people involved in electing its leaders. That is why India is called the **largest democracy**.

Our country has a representative democracy. In this type of a democracy, political parties put up candidates for election. The candidate should be at least 25 years old and an Indian citizen. Political parties play a very important part in a democracy. They work as a link between the masses and the government and organize public opinion.

The President is the supreme head of the nation. She/he is elected by the Parliament for a period of five years. The President represents the nation but the real powers are not with him/her. She/he is only a symbolic head and acts on the advice of a council of ministers called the Central Cabinet. The Cabinet is headed by the Prime Minister who has the real powers.

The parliament has two houses of legislature - Lok Sabha (House of the people) and the Rajya Sabha (Council of States).Lok Sabha - the members are directly elected by the people. It has 552 members in total who normally remain for five years after which there is an election. It can be terminated only if the party in power loses its majority. Rajya Sabha - it has a maximum of 250 members. Twelve are nominated or chosen by the President while 238 are indirectly elected by the members of the state legislative assemblies and by the union territories. The members have a term of six years, but they are not all chosen at the same time. One third are elected every two years and at the same time another one third resign. Thus it is a permanent house which is always there.

PRESIDENTS OF INDIA

Rajendra Prasad
(1952-1962)

S. Radhakrishnan
(1962-1967)

Zakir Hussain
(1967-1969)

V. V. Giri
(1969-1974)

Fakhruddin Ali Ahmed
(1974-1977)

N. Sanjeeva Reddy
(1977-1982)

Zail Singh
(1982-1987)

R. Venkataraman
(1987-1992)

S. D. Sharma
(1992-1997)

K. R. Narayanan
(1997-2002)

A. P. J. Abdul Kalam
(2002- 2007)

Pratibha Patil
(2007- 2012)

Pranab Mukherjee
(2012- till date)

PRIME MINISTERS OF INDIA

Jawahar Lal Nehru
(1947-64)

Lal Bahadur Shastri
(1964-66)

Indira Gandhi
(1966-77) (1980-84)

Morarji Desai
(1977-79)

Charan Singh
(1979-80)

Rajiv Gandhi
(1984-89)

V. P. Singh
(1989-90)

Chandra Shekhar
(1990-91)

Narasimha Roa
(1991-96)

Atal Bihari Vajpayee
(1996), (1998-2004)

H. D. Deve Gowda
(1996-97)

I. K. Gujral
(1997)

Manmohan Singh
(2004 till date)

WILDLIFE OF INDIA

Wildlife of India

India's geographical diversity ensures unique wildlife species. Indian wildlife has the uncanny ability to cope with the changing environment. With almost every kind of climatic region, starting from extreme temperature of deserts to sea, rivers, forest and even snow-covered hills, India contains different types of wildlife. With 4% area covered with dense forest, the forest is the prime habitat for wildlife growth and security in India. And it's no wonder, that there are almost 482 sanctuaries and 90 National parks in India for wildlife preservation.

WILDLIFE OF NORTH INDIA

North India is one of the most important habitations of wildlife. Starting from Himalayan range to the northern plains, it gives shelter to a wide range of fauna. Some of the animals that can be spotted are Yaks, Snow Leopard, Red Panda and Mountain Goats.

Yak

The largest animal of this cold desert is the yak (dong), a wild ox. It is a long haired animal found all through the Himalayan region. It is this highly insulated shaggy coat which helps it survive such extreme cold. Even with a life of more than 20 years, there may be less than a couple of thousand wild yaks left. The yak has very large, thick horns that can reach a length of 40 inches in male yaks. Yaks have been domesticated in Ladakh for thousands of years and are a very valuable animal in the Himalayan economy. Smaller domesticated yaks are commonly used for heavy labour, for milk and meat and as a source of wool. Its dung provides fuel in the treeless areas of Ladakh and the Tibetan Plateau. Unfortunately, it is also hunted for its meat and coat.

Species status: Vulnerable

Places to see: Found in the wild in the Ladakh region of Jammu & Kashmir.

FUN FACT
In winter a wild yak can survive temperatures as low as - 40 degrees (F)

Snow Leopard

The strikingly beautiful snow leopard - the big cat of the Himalaya Mountains, is one of the world's most elusive felines. It looks different from the leopard found in more tropical regions with its thick coat of silver grey fur, marked with black spots helping it blend in with the snow covered terrain where it lives. In the wild, Snow leopards can live for about 18 years, while in captivity, their lifespan increases to 20 years. Despite the common misconception, the snow leopard has no relation with the leopard. In fact, some people believe that it has a close connection with the cheetah. Snow Leopards can leap farther than any other cat, reaching distances of well over forty feet in a single bound.

Species status: Endangered

Places to see: Dachigam National Park in Jammu and Kashmir and wildlife

sanctuaries in Darjeeling and the Namdapha National Park in Arunachal Pradesh.

FUN FACT
The snow leopard is incapable of roaring

Red Panda

The Red Panda, also called the Fire Fox or Lesser Panda is a tree dwelling mammal, which looks like a raccoon, with its bushy tail and white and black markings across its face. Characterised by its red fur, the Red Panda looks very different from its larger relative the Giant Panda. Slightly bigger than the domestic cat, the Indian red panda bear is quite good at climbing trees and is mainly herbivorous. Red Pandas are found in North East India - Sikkim, West Bengal and Arunachal Pradesh. The name of a male is referred to as a boar or he-bear while the female is called a sow or she-bear. The lifespan of a Red Panda may range from 9-14 years. Also called Common pandas, Red Pandas are primarily nocturnal creatures found resting in tree branches and hollows during the day. Red Pandas spend most of their time, up to 13 hours a day, foraging for bamboo. The main reason for the declining population is the disintegration of its natural habitats, along with its specific diet needs.

Species status: Endangered

Places to see: Wildlife sanctuaries of Darjeeling, West Bengal and Sikkim

FUN FACT
Red Pandas eat about 80 pounds of bamboo daily. They are also the state animal of Sikkim

Cashmere goat

The goat may be a funny animal to look at, but no one laughs at the Cashmere goat, for it gives us the softest, most expensive wool in the world! It is one of a long-haired breed of goat raised in Tibet and the higher elevations of China, the Indian subcontinent, Afghanistan, and Turkey for its meat, milk, and cashmere wool. Cashmere wool grows as the goat's winter undercoat, which is then covered by a second layer of coarser hair, called guard hair. The outer coat isn't worth much, but the under coat called pashm is. Pashm (Persian word for Wool) or pashmina (Persian/Urdu word driven from Pashm) is known for its use in the handmade shawls of Kashmir. It takes the fleece of 10 cashmere goats to make a shawl a yard and a half square. Each goat produces 3 to 8 ounces of cashmere per year. It takes at least 4 years for a goat to produce the fibre required to make single child apparel.

Species status: Protected

Places to see: Jammu & Kashmir

FUN FACT
The word cashmere derives from an old spelling of Kashmir.

Asiatic or Siberian Ibex

'Ibex' is from the Latin word meaning 'wild goat of the Alps'. Found in Afghanistan, China, India, Kazakhstan, Kyrgyzstan, Mongolia, Pakistan, and Russia, Ibex are a kind of mountain goat. They have huge back-curving horns which are used to defend themselves against predators. The male ibex horns can grow to 28 - 55 inches in length while female horns are slightly shorter, thinner and curve slightly more backwards. The male ibex has a beard on his chin. Ibexes are remarkably sure-footed and agile with splits in their hooves enabling them to leap about rocky ledges. Ibex have been hunted as trophies and for meat and medicinal purposes. The ibex have a lifespan of around 20 years.

Species status: Endangered

Places to see: Herds of Ibex are seen migrating in the glacier zone in summers at the Manali Sanctuary in Himachal Pradesh.

FUN FACT
In an ancient Egyptian recipe for the cure for baldness, ibex fat was included among its ingredients.

Kashmir Markhor

The magnificent spiral-horned Markhor is the largest member of the goat family in the world. The name Markhor probably arose as a derivation of the Pushto words 'mar' (meaning snake) and 'akhur' (meaning horn) - an apt description of the serpentine shape of their horns. This is a very peculiar name, as they are vegetarians, though they have been known to kill snakes. The Markhor is a goat-antelope found in sparse woodland in the Western Himalayas and was highly prized by British 'sportsmen' as a trophy. In Kashmir, the Pir Panjal Markhor is found only in the Pir Panjal Range. In the wild they can live up to 12 years and around 20 years in captivity.

Species status: Endangered

Places to see: It can be spotted in Hirapora Wildlife Sanctuary, Jammu and Kashmir and in the Western Himalayas.

FUN FACT
They are known to climb trees in search for nutritious leaves.

Musk Deer

Musk deer comprise of one of the most endangered deer species, not only in the Indian subcontinent, but also in the whole world. Musk deer resemble small deer with a stocky build, and hind legs longer than their front legs. The Indian Musk deer resembles medium-high dogs in size. Unlike other deer, musk deer do not have antlers, but they have elongated upper canine teeth. Extremely secretive and solitary animals, they are especially active at night-time. They are recognizable by their distinctive jumping movement - more like the steps of a kangaroo than a deer. This species is endangered because of being highly poached for their musk.

Species status: Endangered

Places to see: Can be seen in Kashmir, Kumaon and Sikkim. Kishtwar National Park of Jammu and Kashmir and Nanda Devi National Park along with Kedarnath Wild Life Sanctuary in Uttarkhand.

FUN FACT
Kasturi is the strong scented secretion found in the rare musk deer used for the most expensive perfumes.

Himalayan Black Bear

Indian black bear, also known as the Asiatic Black Bear, Tibetan black bear, Himalayan black bear and Moon bear is an Asiatic species of medium sized bear with a distinctive white or cream 'V' marking on its chest. Its neck is remarkably thick and its ears large for its size. The claws however are comparatively weak. Black bears have coloured vision and their eyesight is very sharp. They can grow up to 6 feet tall and weigh around 220 pounds. The black bears are decreasing due to rampant deforestation and habitat loss. Asiatic black bears also face threat from farmers, who kill them in order to protect their livestock. They can survive up to 35 years in captivity and 25 years in the wild.

Species status: Vulnerable

Places to see: Found right from Kashmir to Assam in the Himalayan ranges.

FUN FACT
Moon bears construct feeding platforms in trees.

Himalayan Brown Bear

The Himalayan Brown Bear is also known as the Himalayan Red Bear, Isabelline Bear or Dzu-The (in Nepal). The bear is thought to be the source of the legend of the Yeti or the 'Abominable Snowman' as it has often been confused or mistaken for that. Brown bears can be recognized by their most distinctive feature, their shoulder hump. They are the second largest species of bear after the polar bear and are heavier in built and weigh more than the black bear. Its brown coat is recognized in the higher regions of the Himalayas. It hibernates in the winters and comes out once the winters are over.

Species status: Vulnerable

Places to see: Found in the Himalayan region.

FUN FACT
A Black Bear can stand on all fours!

Kashmir Stag

Also called Hangul, this deer is native to India and is the State Animal of Jammu and Kashmir. Hangul is the only surviving race of the Red Deer family of Europe in the sub-continent. The male of the species have long hair along their necks and are known to have magnificent antlers with 11 to 16 points, on the other hand, the female do not have hair or horns. The colour of the Hangul's coat is a brownish red, which is why it is also called Red Deer. However this colour can vary with the season and age of the Hangul. In an older Hangul the coat is a dark brown.

Species status: Endangered

Places to see: Can be seen in Dachigam National Park of Kashmir.

FUN FACT
The Kashmir Stag can stand on all fours and is the state animal for Jammu & Kashmir.

Himalayan Sloth Bear

Disheveled in appearance, the sloth bear leads a reclusive life in India's forests, noisily seeking out insects and fruits. It is recognizable by its long muzzle and their chest is usually marked with a whitish 'V' or 'Y' design. Interestingly its face is without hair and it can close its nostrils, protecting it from dust or insects when raiding termite nests or bee hives. A gap in their teeth enables them to suck up ants, termites, and other insects. A nocturnal animal, the sloth bear sleeps during the day in shallow caves, but does not hibernate.

Species status: Vulnerable

Places to see: It is found throughout India, from the foothills to the southern most end of India. It is also found in Assam.

FUN FACT
Sloth bears are the only bears to carry young on their backs. The Hindi word for bear is 'bhalu' inspired by the name of Rudyard Kipling's bear character 'Baloo' in 'The Jungle Book'.

Lammergeyer or Bearded Vulture

The Lammergeyer or Bearded Vulture is an Old World vulture. Typically lammergeyers nest in caves, ledges and low rocks rising from planes. Unlike most vultures, Lammergeyers do not have a bald head. This huge bird has a large wingspan, and is unlike most other vultures in flight due to its long narrow wings and wedge shaped tail. Like other vultures it is a scavenger, feeding mostly from carcasses of dead animals. It usually avoids rotting meat and lives on a diet that is 90% bone marrow. It will drop large bones from a height to crack them into smaller pieces. Its old name of Ossifrage ('bone breaker') relates to this habit. Live tortoises are also dropped in similar fashion to crack them open. It can live up to 40 years in captivity.

Species status: Protected

Places to see: Found in the Himalayan region and northern mountains.

FUN FACT
The name of the Lammergeyer originates from German Lämmergeier, which means 'lamb-vulture' or 'lamb-hawk'. The name stems from the belief that it attacked lambs.

WILDLIFE OF EAST INDIA

East India is one of the richest regions pertaining to fauna. It is the home of the famous Royal Bengal Tiger found in the Sunderbans, and the one horned Rhino. The eastern part of the country is dotted with thick deciduous forest, which is the home of the wild elephants, spotted deer (chital), leopards, Indian Buffalo (Gaur) and a variety of other animals. Bhitarkanika on the estuary of Mahanadi in Orissa is the sanctuary for the largest estuarine crocodile in the world. Millions of migratory birds fly down to a saltwater lake, called Chilka, in Orissa.

Bengal Tiger

The Royal Bengal tiger is the national animal of India. Like its name, these tigers are mostly found in the state of Bengal and its neighbouring territories. With its orange hide marked with dark stripes, its white underbelly, long tail, huge paws and fearsome teeth, the Royal Bengal Tiger of India is justifiably called the "King of the Jungle." The pattern of stripes on a tiger's skin along with the paw print or pugmark is unique to each tiger and used to identify and track them. Tigers have incredible vision, they can see six times better than humans. Bengal tigers are very adaptable and can live in any habitat. Tigers stalk and pounce because they are unable to chase prey a long distance. A tiger can consume as much as 40kg (88 lb.) of meat in one feeding. They have a life span of 15 years in the wild and can live up to 20 years in captivity.

Another type of tiger called the **White Tiger** is the same as a Royal Bengal Tiger except for a genetic mutation that causes the change in the colour of their fur and eyes. White tigers have blue eyes and brownish stripes.

Species status: Endangered

Places to see: Sariska Tiger Reserve located in Rajasthan, Corbett National Park, Manas National Park, Ranthambore National Park etc.

FUN FACT

All White Tigers in captivity in the world today are the descendants of one white tiger, Mohan, caught by the Maharaja of Rewa in 1951.

Hoolock Gibbon

The Hoolock Gibbon is a tree dwelling ape found in North Eastern India. It is the only ape found in the Indian subcontinent. This ape is characterized by its long hair, curved white brow streaks, and faintly triangular shaped head. Because of its white brows it is also called the 'White Browed Gibbon'. Newborn Gibbons are hairless except for a small clump of hair on their heads. It displays amazing agility in swinging through the trees of the evergreen forests where it lives and makes loud calls, which can be heard through the forest. Hoolocks use their arms to swing through the trees in a rapid movement. On the ground Hoolock Gibbons walk in an upright position on their legs.

Species status: Endangered

Places to see: Found in several states of North East India - Assam, Arunachal Pradesh, Manipur, Meghalaya, Tripura and Nagaland.

DID YOU KNOW?
The arms of Hoolock Gibbons are longer than their legs.

One horn Rhino

The Great Indian Rhinoceros, also called the Greater One-horned Rhinoceros, is characterized by the single horn on its nose and by the loose folds of its thick skin. Indian Rhinoceros holds the distinction of being the fourth largest animal. This species was described by early travelers as a unicorn because of its single horn. The Rhinoceros has a somewhat pre-historic appearance and looks as if it has armour plates, because of the loose folds of its thick hide. The Indian Rhino differs from its African counterparts as it has a single horn compared to the two horns of the African Rhino. Despite its heavy body, the Indian Rhinoceros can still run at a speed of more than 55 kilometers per hour and can even swim. A fully grown male rhino weighs over 2000kgs. Their eyesight is comparatively poor. The Great Indian Rhinoceros is herbivorous and do not prey on animals. The only time they are known to kill is if they are fighting for their territory. Rhinos live for 30-45 years in the wild and have been recorded as living up to 47 years in captivity.

Species status: Endangered

Places to see: Can be seen in the Kaziranga and Manas wildlife sanctuaries in Assam in North East India.

Gaur/Bison

The Gaur or Indian Bison is the largest wild cattle. In the North East, a domesticated Gaur known as Mithun is used as a farm animal and is sacrificed and eaten at ritual feasts. Gaur are said to look like water buffalo from the front and domestic cattle from the back. The horns are present at the side of the head and curve upwards. They are herbivorous and live in grassy clearings and in evergreen and deciduous forests. It can live in altitudes up to 1,800 m. Gaurs usually live in herds of around 10 animals that are led by an adult male bull. They spend the night in a forest and emerge into the forest clearings to feed during the day. They are known to have killed tigers while protecting themselves.

Species status: Vulnerable

Places to see: Nagarhole and Bandipur National Parks in Karnataka India, and Kaziranga and Manas National Parks in Assam in North East India.

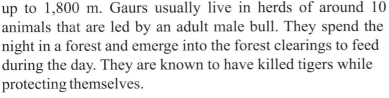

Chital /Deer

Deer are one of the most beautiful creatures on this earth and extend to approximately 34 species. Male deer are known as stags, harts, bucks or bulls, depending upon their species, while the females are known as hinds, does or cows. One of the many species of Deer is the Axis Deer, also known as Chital Deer or Spotted Deer, native animal of the Indian subcontinent. Its antlers, which it sheds annually, are usually three-pronged and curved. The spotted deer is found in large numbers in dense deciduous or semi-evergreen jungles and open grasslands. Their life expectancy ranges from 20-30 years. Their diet consists of all kinds of vegetation but grass is the favourite. Surprisingly, they also eat the antlers that they shed for their rich nutrients.

Species status: Protected

Places to see: Spotted deer populations are seen in Corbett, Kanha, Dudhwa, Bandhavgarh, Mudumalai and Sariska.

FUN FACT
The only continents where deer are not found are those of Antarctica and Australia.

Leopard

Leopards are the fifth largest of all cat species. The name 'Leopard' has been derived from a combination of two Greek and Latin words leo and pard, 'leo' meaning lion and 'pard' meaning panther as it is believed that it is a crossbreed between lion and panther. They have a heavy and sturdy body and their head is larger in proportion to their body. The coat of a leopard is covered with rosettes and they can climb trees with effortless ease.

Indian leopards are nocturnal creatures and are considered one of the stealthiest animals. The rare Black Panther, a leopard with a completely black coat, is seen in India. They can easily make themselves undetected, even while living close to human settlements. Leopards are very good swimmers and have an acute sense of hearing, along with sharp eyesight. They are carnivores and eat almost every animal. Injured, sickly or struggling leopards, with a shortage of prey, may even hunt humans. Leopards can live for up to 20 years in the wild and 25 years in captivity.

Species status: Near threatened

Places to see: Ranthambore National Park and Sariska tiger reserve.

FUN FACT
Leopards are the best tree climbers amongst big cats and are capable of taking prey that is twice their body weight, up a tree.

Clouded Leopard

Clouded leopards have a tan or tawny coat, and are distinctively marked with large, irregularly-shaped, dark-edged ellipses which are said to be shaped like clouds. Clouded Leopard is an excellent climber with its short legs and broad paws. It inhabits dense evergreen forests, hunting at night. It has very powerful jaws and big upper canine teeth. It has a life span of 11-17 years.

Species status: Vulnerable

Places to see: It is easily spotted in the Corbett, Namdhapha and Manas National Park in India.

FUN FACT
It is the state animal of Meghalaya.

Gharial

The Gharial or the Indian crocodile is one of two surviving members of the family Gavialidae, a long-established group of crocodile-like reptiles with long, narrow jaws. It is one of the three crocodilians found in India, the others being the Mugger and the Salt water crocodile. The physical attributes of the Gharial do not make it very suited for moving about on land. In fact, the only reason the Gharial leaves the water is either to bask in the sun or to nest on the sandbanks of the river. The species has a characteristic elongated, narrow snout, whose shape varies with the age of the creature. The snout becomes progressively thinner the older the Gharial gets. The length of a Gharial crocodile is somewhere around 5 to 6 meters. It has long and narrow jaws, which are razor-sharp. Young Gharials eat insects, larvae, and small frogs. Mature adults feed almost solely on fish, although some individuals have been known to scavenge dead animals. It is the longest species of crocodiles, some measuring to over 20 feet.

Species status: Critically endangered

Places to see: National Chambal Sanctuary, Katarniaghat Wildlife Sanctuary, Son River Sanctuary and the rainforest biome of Mahanadi in Satkosia Gorge Sanctuary, Orissa.

FUN FACT
The Gharial has 106 to 110 teeth in the snout.

WILDLIFE OF SOUTH INDIA

The hot and humid climate of South India with thick forests has rare wildlife such as wild elephants, deer, pythons, and venomous snakes. Southern India has the dense concentration of King Cobra, the largest venomous snake in the world. There are more types of birds than animals in this part of the region.

Asian Elephant

Their height, weight and strength are almost legendary. Elephants have been around for almost 40 million years now. The average life expectancy of an elephant in the wild is 60-70 years, whereas it is around ten more in captivity. In the final stages of its life, the longevity of its life depends on its teeth. Elephants go through 6 sets of molars during their life span. The first set of teeth is pushed out by the new set at the age of 2. It is the fourth set at the age of 20 - 25 that is their first set of adult teeth. They get their last set around the age of 60. Once this last set wears out and the elephant can no longer eat, it dies. Interestingly, elephants rest in a standing position or while reclining on their side. It consumes a whopping average of 300 litres of water a day, taking in approximately 60 to 80 litres in a single drink. An elephant bears a child only once in approximately 3-4 years and its gestation period is also extremely long 19-21 months, a record in itself. Elephant families usually consist of 3-10 individuals, where the head of the family is usually an old female who is normally the largest. In India, the elephant is a revered animal, also a part of Indian mythology and religion.

Species status: Endangered

Places to see: The Indian elephant is found in the states of Tamil Nadu, Karnataka, Kerala, Uttar Pradesh, Sikkim, West Bengal, Bihar, Orissa and Assam.

FUN FACT
Elephants walk on their toes!

Indian Cobra Snake

Also called King Cobra it is the longest species of venomous snake. It is one of the big four members which is responsible for causing the most snakebite cases in India. In a single bite it can inject enough venom to kill an elephant, around 6-7 ml. This is enough to kill up to 20 people. When threatened, the King Cobra reacts by putting on a threat display because of which its hood looks very distinctive and impressive. Cobras normally feed on rodents, toads, frogs, birds and snakes. Its diet of rats leads it to areas inhabited by humans including farms and outskirts of urban areas. The King cobra kills by striking its prey with its fangs and injecting a lethal amount of venom. It then swallows its prey whole. They can live up to 20 years in the wild.

Species status: Protected

Places to see: Snake Park in Chennai, Tamil Nadu and sanctuaries in South and North Eastern India

FUN FACT

King Cobras are the only snake in the world that build a nest for their young, just like a bird, but on the ground!

Rock Pythons

Rock Python snake, also known as *Ajgar*, is one of the most massively built snakes of the Indian subcontinent. It belongs to the Boidae Family and is dependent on water to quite an extent. One of the unique features of the Rock pythons of India is that they can raise their body temperature above the surrounding level, through muscular contractions. This snake grows to an average length of around 4 meters. The entire body is covered with scales, which are usually smooth and glossy. Indian rock pythons kill by biting and constricting the rodents and other small mammals they catch. They then swallow the prey whole, though it's often many times larger than the snake's own head. After eating a huge meal, they may go without food for many days. There is also an incidence of an Indian python not eating for 2 years at a stretch. Their lifespan is between 20-30 years.

FUN FACT

The pythons manage a miraculous feat of eating something bigger than their size by dislocating their jaw and stretching its elastic skin around the unfortunate victim.

Species status: Endangered

Places to see: Found throughout the Indian subcontinent from Kashmir to Kanyakumari.

Saltwater Crocodile

It is the largest of all living reptiles. The male saltwater crocodiles can reach lengths of 23 feet and females of over 10 feet. As its name implies, this species is found in salty waters around coastal areas and in rivers. Adult saltwater crocodiles are a dark colour with occasional tan or yellow spots. The underbelly is a pale white colour. This is a large headed species with a heavy set of jaws. These crocodiles cannot open their mouth if it is held closed, even with the help of an adhesive tape. Its typical hunting technique is known as the 'death roll': it grabs onto the animal and rolls powerfully in the water. Saltwater crocodiles are meat eaters. Each crocodile jaw has 24 sharp teeth, used for grasping and crushing, but not chewing. The teeth of a crocodile get replaced throughout its life. They will eat snakes, buffaloes and domestic cattle. Adult crocodiles have no natural enemies and are capable of bringing down prey as large as an adult Asian water buffalo. Crocodiles sweat through their mouth and the gesture of lying with their mouth wide open is just a way to cool off.

Species status: Endangered

Places to see: The saltwater crocodile has a vast geographical range that extends from Cochin on the west coast of India to the Sunderbans in West Bengal and to the Andaman Islands.

FUN FACT
The back skin of a crocodile can deflect arrows, spears and even bullets!

WILDLIFE OF CENTRAL INDIA

Central India houses some of the best wildlife sanctuaries such as Kanha and Bandhavgarh, which are well known for their tiger population. The immense natural beauty of Kanha even inspired the famous author Rudyard Kipling to write his all time classic Jungle Book. Some rare animals such as the Indian Wolf, four-horned antelopes are also found there.

Indian Wolf

Indian wolves do not form large packs like other wolves, though they tolerate crowding conditions in captivity better. Packs typically consist of a family of six to eight animals, though pairs are more common. They tend to breed from mid-October to late December. The cubs are born blind with floppy ears and a white mark on the chest which disappears with age. Indian wolves are generally smaller than European wolves, being 3 feet in length and 26 inches high at the shoulder, while the tail is 16 to 18 inches long. They typically prey on antelopes, rodents and hares. They usually hunt in pairs when targeting antelopes.

Species status: Endangered

Places to see: Indian Wolf is mainly distributed across the states of Gujarat, Rajasthan, Haryana, Uttar Pradesh, Madhya Pradesh, Maharashtra, Karnataka and Andhra Pradesh

FUN FACT
The Indian wolf is said to be the main ancestors of the domestic dogs.

Four-Horned Antelopes

Four Horned Antelope or Chousingha is half a meter tall and weighs around 20 kgs. This four-horned antelope with a dark coat is rarely found far from water, and must drink regularly in order to survive. Male Chousingha grow four horns, two between the ears and the second pair right on the front of the fore head. Four Horned Antelopes prefer living in terrestrial, dry deciduous forests, wooded areas rich in vegetation near streams or rivers. They feed on grasses, shoots, fruits, leaves and other vegetations. Their life span is approximately 10 years.

Species status: Vulnerable

Places to see: Tamil Nadu and Orissa. They can also be spotted at the Corbett, Bandipur, Sariska, Nagarhole and Kanha National Parks in India.

FUN FACT
The world's only wild creature with two pair of horns, Chowsingha (Four horned antelope) is found in Sariska.

Blackbuck

Blackbuck or Krishna Mrigam is a species of antelope found mainly in India. It is one of the fastest of all terrestrial animals reaching to speeds of up to 80 km/h and is one of the few antelopes where males and females have distinctive coloration, as the male bucks are black and white and have long twisted horns, while females are fawn coloured with no horns. The maximum life span recorded is 16 years and the average is 12 years.

Species status: Near threatened

Places to see: Found in various National Parks like Velavadar Blackbuck National Park, Bandhavgarh, Kanha, Ranthambore, Corbett, Bharatpur Bird Sanctuary and Gir.

FUN FACT
It is the state animal of Andhra Pradesh. The blackbuck was kept as a pet by Indian royalty, and tame individuals roamed freely around temples

Even with its arid climatic condition West India has a wide variety of fauna. Along with the tiger reserve of Ranthambore, this western sector provides the only home for the Asiatic Lion. Birds are one of the most important fauna found in this region. Apart from Peacocks, the national bird, migratory birds fly down here every winter. Keola Deo Ghana bird sanctuary is a rare treat for every traveler. This region also houses big antelopes such as the Sambar Deer and the Neelgai.

FUN FACT
The lion's tail is the only one in the cat family with a tassel at the tip. Lion cubs are born blind.

Asiatic Lion

Asiatic Lion is the second largest 'Big Cat' in the world, after the ferocious tiger. The Ashoka Pillar, the national emblem of India, depicts three snarling Asiatic lions as well. Indian Lions are the only Big Cats that are seen living in large groups, known as 'prides'. The males are orange-yellow to dark brown in colour, while the females have a sandy or tawny colour. Males also have a mane, which is usually dark in colour, but rarely black. This characteristic mane is absent in the females. They are found inhabiting open grasslands and forests. Asiatic Lions are highly endangered species and have become extinct from all the countries of the world, except the Indian subcontinent. In India also, the animal is found only in the Gir forests of Gujarat. A lion's lifespan is 15 years in the wild.

Species status: Endangered

Places to see: Gir Reserve Forest in Gujarat.

Sambar Deer

Sambar deer is prevalent in almost every corner of India, but is mainly found in central India. Sambar deer stands to a height of 135-150 cm at the shoulder and can weigh up to 300kg. Males have antlers measuring up to one meter. Its coat is dark brown in colour. It is characterized with large muzzle and broad ears. It has thick fur and orange spots on its body. Males are larger than the females and have thick mane of hairs around the neck. Sambar Deer prefer marshy and wooded areas to live. They feed on leaves, vegetation, herbs, fruit, bamboo buds and mushrooms. They have an average life span of 8 to 12 years in the wild and around 25 years in captivity.

Species status: Vulnerable

Places to see: Found in many national parks like Kanha, Jim Corbett, Ranthambore, Bandhavgarh, Gir, Manas, Kaziranga and Sariska.

FUN FACT
At the sight of a predator, the Sambar Deer tends to alertly watch and keep giving alarm calls until the danger has passed, hence getting killed often.

Peacocks

The Indian peacock is the national bird of India. It is a colourful, swan-sized bird, with a fan-shaped crest of feathers, a white patch under the eye and a long, slender neck. According to Greek Mythology, the peacock was a physical representation of Hera, Queen of the Gods. Indian Peacock do most of their foraging in the early morning and shortly before sunset. Peacock feathers are popular decorations and often used in crafts. Peacocks retreat to the shade and security of the forest for the hottest portion of the day. Foods include grains, insects, small reptiles, small mammals, berries, drupes, wild figs, and some cultivated crops. The chick of a peacock can walk, eat and drink on its own, even when it is hardly a day old Peacocks have an average lifespan of twenty years in the wild.

Species status: Protected

Places to see: The Indian Peacock lives primarily south to east of the Indus River including Kashmir, Jammu, east Assam, south Mizoram, and the entire Indian peninsula.

FUN FACT
A group of peacocks is referred to as a party!

Neelgai

The largest Asiatic antelope, Neelgai is found throughout the Indian state of Haryana and the males which appear ox-like are also known as Blue bulls. Neelgai is 6-7 feet long and weighs around 120-240 kg. They are 4-5 feet tall and males have 8-10 inch long horns. Male coats are greyish blue and female coats are yellowish brown in colour. Neelgai prefer to live in open plains, woodlands, dense jungles and grasslands and generally come to the same place to deposit their droppings. They can go days without water and feed on plants, seeds, branches, leaves, fruit, flowers, stems and buds. The local belief, that Neelgai are a cow and hence sacred, has protected it against hunting. The life span for Neelgai is around 21 years.

Species status: Low risk

Places to see: Karanataka, West Bengal, Assam, Rajasthan.

FUN FACT
In fact Neelgai were known as the Nilghor (nil = blue, ghor = horse) during the rule of Aurangzeb.

Wild Water Buffalo

The water buffalo, or Asian buffalo, as it is often called, is the largest member of the Bovini tribe. Adult water buffalo range in size from 400 to 900 kg and in the wild, water buffalo can weigh up to 1,200kg, while females are about two-thirds this size. Around 95% of the world's total water buffalo population is found in Asia, with India being the home of half of them. Also known as a swamp buffalo, the water buffalo is black or white in colour, sometimes both, and has gently curved sweptback horns. The horns can be as long as 3 meters long. Females normally produce calves every other year, after a gestation of 9 to 11 months. Water buffalo have been domesticated for more than 5,000 years.

FUN FACT
The domesticated water buffalo is often referred to as the 'living tractor of the East,' as it is relied upon for plowing and transportation in many parts of Asia.

Species status: Endangered

Places to see: Chhatisgarh and Assam

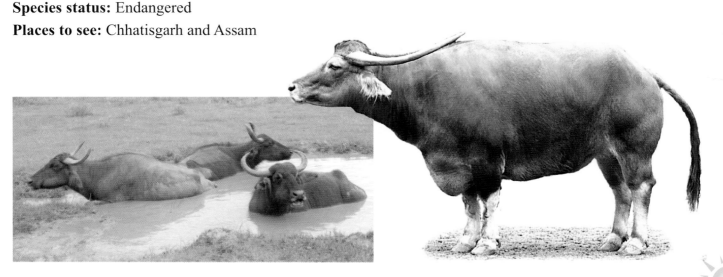

Indian Camel

Long-curved neck, deep-narrow chest and a single hump characterize the Indian camel. They are known as the 'Ship of the Desert'. The hump is used by the camels as reservoir of fatty tissues and in times of scarcity, the camel receives energy from them. Indian Camel is 6 feet long and weighs around 700kg. They are usually brown or black in colour. Camel's nasal passages are properly covered with the large muscular nostrils. Camels have thin, long and powerful legs. They also have large eyes with long eyelashes and bushy eyebrows, but small ears. Indian camels have broad, flat and leathery pads with two toes on each foot with leathery patches on their knees. Camels are herbivorous and feed on grass, grains, wheat, oats, dried leaves, and seeds. As their humps contain fat, they can go without food for 3-4 days.

The other type of camel found in India is the double humped camel called Bactrian camel found in the northern Ladakh regions. It is believed that these camels were domesticated before 2500 BC. The temperature in deserts where these camels live rises to about 38° C in the summer and falls to as low as -29° C in the winter. Bactrian camels adapt to both the extremes of climatic conditions. A very thirsty camel can drink up to 135 liters of water in just 13 minutes. At one time, it can drink water up to 30 percent of its body weight.

In order to prevent sand from entering their nose, the camels have the ability to close their nostrils.

Species status: Bactrian camels are endangered

Places to see: Single humped camels can be found in Rajasthan, double humped in Ladakh region of Jammu & Kashmir.

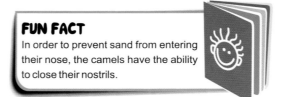

FUN FACT
In order to prevent sand from entering their nose, the camels have the ability to close their nostrils.

Overall, Indian wildlife is highly diverse, and it changes according to the climatic condition and vegetation. India is blessed with a unique and extremely rich and varied flora and fauna. It boasts of around 88 National Parks and 490 Wildlife Sanctuaries, sheltering over 390 mammals, 455 reptiles, 210 amphibians, 1,230 bird species and 30,000 species of insects, making the country one of the most sought after wildlife destinations in the world.

Tell me about
MAHABHARATA

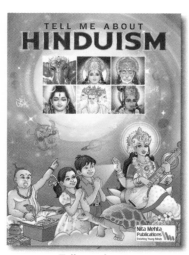

Tell me about
HINDUISM

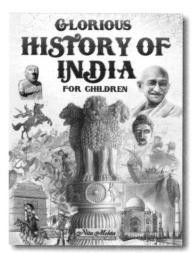

Glorious HISTORY of India
for Children

India after INDEPENDENCE
for children

Tell me about
SIKH GURUS

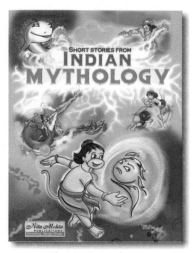

Short Stories from
INDIAN MYTHOLOGY

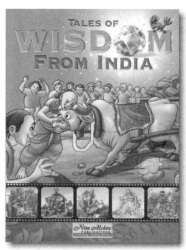

Tales of WISDOM
from India

Tell me about
RAMAYANA

Tell me about
HINDU GODS & GODDESSES

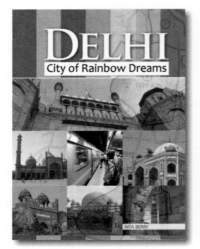